ONE THING FIRST

Pursuing Spiritual Intimacy with God

BRIDGETTE SIMS

outskirts
press

One Thing First
Pursuing Spiritual Intimacy with God
All Rights Reserved.
Copyright © 2020 Bridgette Sims
v4.0

The opinions expressed in this manuscript are solely the opinions of the author and do not represent the opinions or thoughts of the publisher. The author has represented and warranted full ownership and/or legal right to publish all the materials in this book.

This book may not be reproduced, transmitted, or stored in whole or in part by any means, including graphic, electronic, or mechanical without the express written consent of the publisher except in the case of brief quotations embodied in critical articles and reviews.

Outskirts Press, Inc.
http://www.outskirtspress.com

ISBN: 978-1-9772-1730-1

Cover Photo © 2020 www.gettyimages.com. All rights reserved - used with permission.

Outskirts Press and the "OP" logo are trademarks belonging to Outskirts Press, Inc.

PRINTED IN THE UNITED STATES OF AMERICA

Table of Contents

Introduction I

One Thing 1

The Call 7

Dinner Is Served 11

Be. Here. Now. 15

Do the Right Thing 20

One Day at a Time 24

Our Daily Bread 29

Fear Not! 32

Is Something Burning? 36

Arise and Eat 40

Shut the Door 44

Divine Favor 47

Changed in His Presence 51

I Will Give You Rest 55

Jesus Satisfies	59
It's Going to Rain	63
Ride or Die	66
Overcharged	71
Seeking for Jesus	76
Don't Hide	82
Loving People, Loving Him	85
Starting Over	89
Follow Me	94
Seasons Change	98
In the House	102
Say Yes!	106
When God Is Silent	109
In Pursuit	113
Scriptures	119
Beginning a New Life in Christ	122

Introduction

Luke 10:38–42

Luke 10:42: "One thing is needful …"

Martha and Mary. Sisters in contrast. Mary sits at Jesus' feet to listen to him. Martha is busily working and distracted. In her frustration, she appeals to Jesus. She says, "Lord, don't you care that my sister has left me to serve alone? Tell her to help me!"

The entire episode plays out in Scripture in five verses. Yet Jesus' response touches on the core issue of many believers in Christ: "Martha, Martha, you are worried and troubled about many things. But one thing is needed, and Mary has chosen that good part, which will not be taken away from her."

For many years of my Christian walk I have desired to make spending time with Jesus my priority. Too often, though, I have worn Martha's shoes. I know I'm not alone. I believe Mary and Martha personify two warring parts in the life of every believer. We want to seek God with all our heart, mind, and soul as He commands. We want desperately to be close to Him, to sit at His feet and hear His voice speaking to our heart. Yet, every day we allow ourselves to be swept away by the tide called life! Having consistent time alone with God can be a real struggle in the age of instant messaging, texting, social networking, and the like. Despite all this, His words ring true now more than ever before. "One thing is needed ..."

During this brief snapshot in her life, Jesus commends Mary for making the right choice among many. After all, there were other important things she *could* have been doing that day ...

There is always more to do.

There are calls to make, appointments to attend, and people to see. Your job and your family make demands of you. Church life alone can present an entirely separate set of requests and requirements. There is no absence of activities we could be involved in. The pull we feel daily is the same pull Mary and Martha felt. When reading this story in Scripture, you get the feeling that there are a lot of things going on and a lot of things that need to get done. Martha got to work. It seemed like the obvious thing to do.

Both women loved the Lord. They just made different choices.

Jesus says one thing matters. One thing takes precedence over all else. Only one thing is of vital necessity, and that is, *spending time with Him*.

One day, while I was spending time with the Lord, He impressed this thought upon my heart: "Of all the things you have to do today, this is the most important."

That statement is true every day of our lives. I don't know about your job, your family life, or the many roles you play. I don't know what your responsibilities are. I do know this: it is important that you spend time with the Lord daily. It is important for every believer.

In Psalm 27:4, David said, "One thing have I desired of the Lord and that will I seek after; that I may dwell in the house of the Lord all the days of my life, to behold the beauty of the Lord, and to enquire in His temple." David wants one thing here. His desire is to be in the presence of the Lord, spending time with Him, talking and listening to Him. There were so many other things he could have asked for. There were other things he could have pursued. He chose this one thing.

This book is about one thing. THE one thing. The main thing. Pursuing spiritual intimacy with Christ.

This is not a how-to on having quiet time with God, although we will touch on that. Let's go beyond quiet time and explore different aspects of the subject of spiritual intimacy with God through the pages of Scripture. This is a drop in a very deep well, but it's a place to begin the journey.

Don't attempt to race through this book. I do that when I'm reading sometimes because I want to hurry and get to the end. Meditate on each Scripture focus and the accompanying Scriptures within the devotional. Let each devotional marinate in your heart and mind. Ask the Lord to show you how they relate to you specifically. Some readings will resonate with you more, depending on the season you are in now, than others. Take your time.

This is a process. Spiritual intimacy—that is, walking closely in fellowship with God—doesn't happen overnight. I certainly don't have all the answers, but I would like to share what I have been learning with you. Reflect on your own experiences in your walk with Him and think about what He has been teaching you. There is contact information at the end of this book. Please let me know what you are learning too.

As you read these pages, I pray that you will agree with Jesus and declare that yes, one thing is needful.

I pray that you will say with David, "One thing have I desired of the Lord and that will I seek after ..."

I pray that you will seek to make your personal relationship with Christ of utmost priority.

I pray that time with God will not be a check-off on a to-do list, but a precious time of fellowship with the One who loves and cares for you like no other: He is Jesus. He is King of Kings, Lord of Lords, the Wonderful Counselor, the Savior, and the Almighty God.

I pray that you crave His presence more than anything else in this world.

I have not arrived in my quest to be as close to God as possible, but to borrow the words of Paul in Philippians 3:14, "I press toward the mark for the prize of the high calling of God in Christ Jesus."

Will you join me?

―――――――

Dear reader, I pray that if you do not know Jesus Christ as your Lord and Savior you will accept His death and resurrection as payment for your sins. There is more information about this at the end of the book. I pray that you will grow in leaps and bounds in the grace and knowledge of Him.

If you have accepted Jesus as Lord and Savior, I pray that your walk with the Lord will move into greater dimensions than you ever imagined possible. He is able to do "… Exceeding abundantly above all that (you) ask or think according to the power that works in (you)" (Ephesians 3:20).

I pray that you walk in close fellowship with Him every day of your life. May your life be marked by unwavering faithfulness and obedience to His Word. I pray that you walk in uncompromising boldness and in the full authority of God as you grow in Him. I believe the Holy Spirit will cause you to recognize anything in your life that would hinder or negatively affect your relationship with Him. I pray that you are sensitive to the Spirit. I pray you repent and make the needed changes quickly. I pray you live in such a way that He is not grieved. Precious reader, I pray your walk with the Lord is not the same. May you experience an intimate closeness with God unsurpassed by anything the world could attempt to offer. In Jesus' Name I pray – Amen.

One Thing

Psalm 27

"One thing have I desired of the Lord and that will I seek after ..." (Psalm 27:4)

Pursuing spiritual intimacy with God requires single-minded focus.

Psalm 27:4 is my core Scripture. Over the years it has been my compass in my walk with the Lord. I have found that when I am closest to God, I am intentionally focused on walking this Scripture out. When it is not in the forefront of my mind, I drift away from Him. Other, less important things crowd in and rise to the top place of prominence in my heart.

"One thing have I desired of the Lord ..."

One thing.

We live in a multitasking society. We like to boast about the fact that we can do several things at once.

Why are cell phones and other electronics upgraded so often? It's because we like our stuff to be able to do more than one thing at a time. Developers are just trying to keep up with our demands.

There are lots of times when multitasking is required. I have found, though, that I don't always do it well. It can be difficult and frustrating doing several things at once. When I attempt *serious* multitasking, there is a chance that something is lacking.

I could never be a chef. Yes, I know we can do all things through Christ Jesus. It would require the overflowing anointing of Jesus for *me* to be a chef!

A great chef or cook prepares several items for a meal at the same time. Each item may require different temperatures for cooking, different means of preparation, different utensils, etc. Chefs are great at multitasking. Often, when I prepare several items for a meal, something boils over, something is burnt, one item is hot and two are cold (when they are supposed to be hot!). I can't tell you how many times I have placed something on the stove or in the oven to cook while I did something else and simply forgot it was there until I smelled it burning. There are times in life when it's better for me to give my full attention to one thing at a time.

That's where David is.

He wants one thing from the Lord.

No multitasking.

No list of lofty goals to accomplish.

He has one focal point.

One thing.

In Scripture, the theme of the "one thing" is repeated more than once …

"Then Jesus beholding him loved him, and said unto him, **one thing** thou lackest …" (Mark 10:21)

"Brethren, I count not myself to have apprehended: but this **one thing** I do …" (Philippians 3:13)

"But beloved, be not ignorant of this **one thing** …" (2 Peter 3:8)

There is power in focusing on <u>one thing</u>!

When God points out a "one thing," He is saying all the other stuff is okay but here is where you need to expend your energy. Here's your breakthrough spot. Get this together and you're on your way. Pay attention here!

Jesus said, "No man can serve two masters: for either he will hate the one and love the other; or else he will hold to the one and despise the other." (Matthew 6:24)

"No man can serve two masters …" In a broader sense, think about masters as being your priorities. You can't make more than one thing the priority in your life. You can't say "These things are the number-one thing in my life." It doesn't make sense.

One thing must outweigh all others.

Imagine David praying before the Lord and sifting through all the thoughts in his head. He declares: *"One thing I ask from the Lord, this only do I seek: that I may dwell in the house of the Lord all the days of my life, to gaze on the beauty of the Lord and to seek him in his temple."*

To me he is saying, Lord, out of everything, there is one thing I need more than anything else.

You.

To be in Your presence.

To seek Your face.

To talk with You.

One thing.

The first step in this journey is determining what's most important to you.

Once the Lord becomes our "one thing," everything else falls in line.

What do you want most of all?

Spiritual intimacy with God will require that everything else is secondary to your relationship with Him.

Everything.

"But I have a job, family, and responsibilities!" you might say. I know. I do too. God knows that and He does not want us to neglect any of those.

God is saying, "Make Me your focus. Put Me first. As you do that, I can help you with your job, show how to love and minister to your family, and I can help you complete your daily responsibilities in a way that glorifies Me. I'll show you what's most important daily and give you wisdom to help you along the way."

There are times when I am in prayer, talking to the Lord, that I rush in with a list of stuff I want. It's then that I hear in my spirit, "One thing I have desired of the Lord and that will I seek after ..."

My prayer shifts. Lord, I want more of You. I want to be closer to You than I am now.

I have said this with a heavy heart sometimes because there were other things that I wanted more. There are things that I think will make me happy; things that will make me feel more fulfilled. I recognize there are things that I desire solely independent of Him. Not Thy will, Lord, but my will be done! My idols don't sit on shelves in a room. They are alive and well and they fight for the supreme seat in my heart.

There is a war going on. I constantly ask the Lord to help me want Him more than anything.

How about you?

What one thing is more important to you than anything else? What do you think about a lot? What do you clear your schedule for? Where do you invest your time and resources?

We can't multitask here. There's no "God and ..." The first step in walking closer to God is desiring Him above all else.

We want our one thing to be ... Jesus.

Making the Lord our one thing will require self-reflection. Ask God to show you the idols in your heart—that is, the things that you love and desire more than being close to Him. He will. One example may be your career. Perhaps your identity and self-worth are tied to your position. You may have chosen (consciously or not) to put your work above everything else. Perhaps your quest for money leaves no time for God. Maybe your love of ministry has overshadowed your love for God. It could be you are overly concerned about your reputation. You don't want to be known as a "church girl or boy" so you downplay and deny your relationship with Him around your peers. These are just examples. God will show you what is going on with you specifically. Once He does, repent. Tell Him you want Him to be King in your heart! Ask Him to help you desire Him more than anything else. We can't love Him without His help. He will do it!

"O Lord, you have examined my heart and know everything about me. You know when I sit down or stand up. You know my thoughts even when I'm far away." (Psalm 139:1,2)

"Search me, O God, and know my heart: test me, and know my anxious thoughts. Point out anything in me that offends you and lead me along the path of everlasting life." (Psalm 139:23–24 NLT)

"Therefore, I tell you, whatever you ask for in prayer, believe that you have received it, and it will be yours." (Mark 11:24)

The Call

Mark 3:13–19

"And He ordained twelve, that they should be with Him ..." (Mark 3:14)

God calls each of us to spiritual intimacy with Him—first!

God uses ordinary people.

Think about it for a minute.

Jesus chose and empowered twelve men with all kinds of personal issues, backgrounds, and vocations to:

- Preach
- Have power to heal sickness and
- Cast out demonic spirits

There were no rulers in the bunch. None of them were graduates from Jerusalem International Seminary. Nonetheless, the ways in which God uses these men is no less than amazing.

How did they go from being tax collectors, fishermen, and the like to becoming *fishers of men*? How were people healed just by being in *their shadow*?

What happened to them?

They answered <u>The Call</u>.

And He ordained twelve, **"that they should be with Him …"**

They were ordained, that is, set apart to *be with Jesus*.

"Follow Me … ," He said. Talk with Me, spend time with Me, watch what I do, pray with Me.

They were called to spiritual intimacy!

The disciples had the amazing opportunity to personally ask Jesus questions about things He said, taught, and did. He taught them privately, lovingly, and patiently, as a loving parent teaches a child. They understood, firsthand, His thoughts, feelings, and concerns. They knew the heart of the Master. They ate with Him. They slept where He slept. They went where He went.

They walked with God.

You and I have been called too.

Before we can do great things *for* Him, we must spend time *with* Him, just like the disciples.

The God of the universe, King of Kings and Lord of Lords, the great "I AM," desires a close relationship with you and me. One-on-one.

It is mind blowing when you think about it.

The call to walk closely with Christ is the call of anyone who truly seeks to be a disciple of Christ.

It's the call of anyone who has a glimpse of their true condition and desires to be changed to be more like Him.

It's the call of those who want to be used to build His Kingdom and do great things for His glory.

It's a call for everyone, though some will not answer.

Many believers want to preach, teach, heal the sick, lead people to Christ, and do other great things like the early disciples. That's great! I believe every follower of Christ should desire to accomplish amazing things for Him. We should want God to enlarge our territory!

The issue is this. We cannot work powerfully or effectively for the Kingdom of God without His presence being the first and main requirement in our life. Spiritual intimacy with God is the prerequisite for service.

We will not develop the character of Christ, unless we spend time with Him. We can't bear fruit if we are not consistently connected to the vine. (John 15:5)

I know this firsthand and you may know it firsthand too.

I see more every day that my effectiveness in my Christian walk, whether it is in ministry, at home, at work, with my family and friends, or wherever, is dependent on how close I am to Him daily. I can't just study the Scripture to preach or teach a lesson. I study Scripture to know His heart more and to learn about Him. I pray, not because I am required to, but because He desires to talk with me, and He wants me to take time to listen to Him.

How powerful and effective we are in service for God is directly linked to our level of intimacy with Him. We minister (at home or out in the world) out of the overflow of time spent with Him, just like the disciples did.

Yes, you are called.

You're **called to intimacy** with Christ!

_____

Let's pray:

Lord, teach me more about the call to spiritual intimacy. Help me to truly understand that I am called to spend time with You before anything else. Teach me what being with You looks like. Being godly, powerful, and effective in other roles is a direct result of being close to You first. I want to be a living sacrifice, holy and pleasing to You. (Romans 12:1) I want to do great things for Your Kingdom. You promised that You will draw near to me, if I draw near to You. (James 4:8) Show me how to do this. Thank you for calling me to be close to You. Thank you for loving me. In Jesus' Name I pray. Amen.

Dinner Is Served

John 21:1–14

"Jesus saith unto them, 'Come and dine …'" (John 21:12)

God desires uninterrupted, focused time with us.

During the span of our marriage, my husband would periodically tell me that we needed to spend more time together. I, in turn, would spin my head in a Linda Blair/*Exorcist*-type fashion as if to say, "Really?"

For the first 14 years of our marriage, we had no children, so it was he and I together all day, every day. Even after our son was born, we were still together quite often as a family.

One day, he was sitting on the couch and I came and sat next to him. First, we were watching TV together. Then, I turned the TV off and we started talking. The conversation was not earth-shattering, but I gave him my full attention and listened intently as he spoke. I asked questions and genuinely tried to understand what he was saying and why it was important to him.

The Holy Spirit said quietly to me, "This is it. This is what he is talking about."

Yes, we were together a lot, but how often had I really stopped whatever I was doing and focused on him?

How often had I listened to him talk halfheartedly?

How often had we shared our deepest thoughts, one-on-one?

My husband wanted uninterrupted, focused time with me. Why? Because he loved me.

And so it is with God.

When Jesus says, "come and dine," He is inviting us to step away from life's demands to talk, to listen, and to share our thoughts and feelings with Him. This is what we see in the twenty-first chapter of John.

The scene takes place after the crucifixion, death, and resurrection of Jesus. The disciples had run away and were afraid. Peter had denied Jesus, as Jesus said he would.

Things didn't turn out the way the disciples expected, so they went back to what they knew: fishing. Only they can't even get that right.

They don't recognize Jesus when he gives fishing instructions, but they follow His commands. When a miracle happens, they realize, *this man must be Jesus*. (Whenever you see a true miracle, know for sure, it's Jesus!)

He fixes breakfast for them and invites them to eat, talk, rest, and reflect.

He invites you and me to do the same thing as often as we need to.

When you are close to God, you can pour your heart out to the Lord. No holding back. No trying to get the words right. It's just you and Jesus.

Think about special occasions you have shared with your family or friends. How many of those times included or were centered around sharing a meal? What do you remember most? While it may be that special dish that you or someone else prepared that still makes your mouth water, more than likely the fellowship stands out in your mind the most. It's the conversations, the laughter, the being in one another's presence that we think about. Those are special times. *That's what Jesus wants with us.* Fellowship. Talking, listening, sharing; unhurried, relaxed times of being together. The banquet has been prepared and the invitation still stands; come and dine.

Is your stomach rumbling? When was the last time you ate? Sometimes we are malnourished. Maybe we are not eating the right foods. Sometimes we feed too much on junk food from social-networking sites and the internet. I have had to put myself on a phone fast. If I picked up the Bible as often as I picked up my phone, I would have my Triple Doctorate in Theology (if there was such a thing!). I usually know where my phone is, but I may have forgotten where I put my Bible last. I have turned around mid-travels to go home and get my phone. I don't think I have ever turned around to go back home to seek God's guidance for the day because I didn't seek Him before I left. Hmmm ...

When God whispers "come and dine," we say (by our actions), "No thank you, I just had about two hours of surfing cable channels. I'm stuffed!" We're full of empty calories when He has declared, "O taste and see that the LORD is good!" (Psalm 34:8a).

An invitation to dinner is usually reserved for one's closest friends. Jesus calls us "friends". (John 15:13-15) Friends share their hearts with one another. Friends spend time together.

God desires uninterrupted time with you.

Come and dine.

As we seek to become closer to the Lord, it is important that we have dedicated time with Him. We may not be able to sit at His feet for extended periods every day, but we do need to make time in our schedules to "dine" with Him regularly. Look at your schedule for this week. When can you spend 20 or 30 minutes of uninterrupted time with the Lord? When can you spend an hour? Make the sacrifice. Make an appointment to meet with Him. Schedule it like you would any other appointment that is very important to you. Don't let anything else disrupt this time. This is fellowship time. Talk to Him and allow Him to pour into you.

Having *quality* time with the Lord is important. For example, if you are physically tired you may not get much out of your time with Him. Get some rest first. Quality time is more important than length of time. You want to be able to focus when you are with Him.

When you find you have free time available that you hadn't planned on, don't plug in another activity. Spend some of that time with Him. Talk to Him and allow Him to pour into you.

Be. Here. Now.

Psalm 46:10

"Be still and know that I am God …" (Psalm 46:10)

Spiritual intimacy is developed as we tune in to God.

Mindfulness.

1. The quality or state of being conscious or aware of something.
2. A mental state achieved by focusing one's awareness on the present moment.

Mindfulness is a pretty big topic these days. Do an internet search on the topic and all types of videos and articles appear about using mindfulness to be more productive, to lose weight, to strengthen your immune system, and on and on.

It's not a new concept. People have practiced mindfulness for many years in many circles.

I worked for a company once that encouraged practicing mindfulness on the job. After orientation when workers were beginning to settle into their day-to-day job, managers gave the employees a sign to put in their workstation. The sign simply said, "Be. Here. Now." Don't think about what you need to do when you go home. Don't ruminate about the conversation you had yesterday with your friend. Be here now. Focus on the task at hand. For whatever hours you have scheduled today, Be. Here. Now.

When we come into the presence of God, it is important that we are fully present.

When we take time to settle down and get before Him, our thoughts will run all over the place. Even though our body is still, our mind will do cartwheels, backflips, and Chinese acrobatics. Isaiah 26:3 says, "You will keep him in perfect peace all who trust in you, all whose thoughts are fixed on you." How can you still your mind and fix your thoughts on God when you are in His presence?

First, ask the Lord to help you quiet your mind and focus on Him.

In his book *I Will Be Found of You*, Francis Frangipane has a simple solution for a common issue: if a thought comes to your mind to do something while you are trying to focus on God, *write it down*. Then go back to fellowship with God.

Read a portion of Scripture aloud or listen to recorded Scripture.

Imagine someone riding a horse. The horse is galloping at full speed. The rider pulls on the reins around the head of the horse to make the horse slow down and finally stop. Hearing God's Word will help rein in your thoughts.

Spend time worshipping the Lord. Thank Him for all He has done that day or that week. Praise Him in song. Make up your own songs from your heart or sing along with a recording.

It may take time to quiet your mind. Take the time required to shift your focus on the Lord.

I remember once being knee-deep in different Bible translations, commentaries, dictionaries, and the like. I felt a nagging feeling in my spirit, like someone was in the room and they wanted something. At one point, I even looked up and said "What?" to no one in particular. Then I finally got it. The Lord wanted to talk with me. I needed to be still in His presence.

It is important to read Scripture, pray, and sing songs of praise and worship when we are alone with God. It's important, though, not to let study or anything else distract us from the One we are studying about. Imagine someone wanting to talk to you and you were singing and telling them how much you loved them. While that is certainly needed, at some point the person might say, "Can you be quiet for a minute so I can talk to you?" Spiritual disciplines are necessary to cultivate intimacy with God. Doing those things is not spiritual intimacy itself. Going out for a special night with my husband cultivates intimacy between us but it's not intimacy itself. Imagine if, after a night out, I went home and said, "good night!" and didn't say anything else to him? I can promise you that would not go over well.

"Be still and know that I am God." (Psalm 46:10)

If anyone knows about mindfulness, it's the Lord.

In Psalm 8:4, David asks God, "What is man, that you are mindful of Him ...?" God is focused on us. It's not just that He knows we exist. He knows our innermost thoughts. He knows our plans for the day before we do. He knows what we need and what will cause us pain. He is arranging things in our lives, setting up divine appointments, or what some call "chance encounters." He hears us. He sees us. We are His focus all day, every day.

As you come into His presence, think about Him! Ask Him what He desires that day. Ask Him how you can glorify Him. Throughout the day make it a point to specifically tune in to Him. That's all He asks. Don't forget Him after church services are over. Don't forget Him after your quiet time in the morning.

Ever been on a date or out with someone and the person you were with was distracted?

When you are with Him, focus on Him.

Be.   Here.   Now.

Let's review ways that can help you focus on the Lord when you are with Him.

1. Ask the Lord to help you quiet your thoughts as you come into His presence. Ask Him to help you focus on Him. There are two things you can do to help with this:
    a. Tell Him everything that is heavy on your heart. Tell Him about those things that concern you or are bothering you. Release everything to Him. Read Philippians 4:6 and 7 and Psalm 138:8. As you give everything to Him, you can move into His peace.
    b. Write down things to do, ideas, or other thoughts that come across your mind when you sit before Him.
2. Spend time worshipping and praising God.

3. Read a portion of Scripture. Ask the Lord to direct your reading. Ask the Holy Spirit to give you understanding and revelation on how the Scripture reflects the nature of God (who He is, what He likes and doesn't like, etc.).
4. Sit quietly in His presence. Give the Lord time to minister to your heart.

Do the Right Thing

"Mary has chosen the good part ..." (Luke 10:42)

Pursuing a close walk with the Lord will require us to make hard choices.

I once read an article about actor and TV show host Arsenio Hall. In the '80s and '90s, Mr. Hall had a highly rated TV talk show and starred in many successful movies.

In later years, it appeared that he completely dropped off the entertainment map. In the article, he was asked why his career took such a turn. Mr. Hall replied that he'd had a son and he determined he could not raise his son and be an entertainer as well. So, he made a choice. He decided to focus his energies on raising his son.

Mr. Hall stated, "I know I did the right thing by taking time off to raise my son. But it came at a price. I turned down many opportunities over the years because I didn't want to leave him for long periods of time. And in Hollywood, as in any business, the calls stop coming when you don't answer." (*Newsweek*, "Arsenio Hall on Choosing Fatherhood over Fame," 6/11/12)

"I know I did the right thing ... But it came at a price."

Doing the right thing usually comes with a price.

Answering the call to spiritual intimacy with God will require us to make choices.

Hard choices.

Unpopular ones.

The rich young ruler, when asked to sell all he had and follow Christ, declined. That's the last we hear of him in Scripture. (Matthew 19:16–22)

Remember Orpah from the Book of Ruth? When given the opportunity, she declined to follow Naomi unto new territory—God's territory. Orpah made the decision to return to her people and her gods. (Ruth 1:15)

Throughout Scripture, when Jesus said, "Follow Me," some said, "No."

It is the same today.

God whispers, "Spend time with Me." How do we respond?

In order to have a close relationship with God, we will be required to choose whether we will sacrifice time to spend with Him, when our schedule may already be set to maximum overload.

We will need to choose to be still before Him when other important things are crying out for our attention.

We will need to make choices like this every day.

Mary chose to be with Jesus. Jesus said, "she *chose* the good part ..."

Remember, though: doing the right thing usually comes with a price!

Know this for a fact: when you determine to focus on cultivating a closer relationship with God, all types of needs will come to the surface. People and situations will begin to make demands on you as never before.

You will be called upon to make unpopular choices.

I can only imagine how people felt when Jesus stole away from the crowds to be with His Father and they couldn't find Him. "He's gone? Where is He? We need Him! We've walked for miles ..."

You can expect to experience the disapproval, disappointment, or anger of those that don't understand your decision to steal away and spend time with the Lord when they would prefer you do something else, like Mary experienced from Martha.

I can't tell you the number of times God has awakened me so I could spend time with Him, and I have chosen to go back to sleep. My flesh wins. There's not enough time to tell you about all the times I have chosen to do something else when I know He desires fellowship with me. I choose the lesser thing. "I'll spend time with You later," I say. Only later does not come. I may be doing other good things, but the good is truly the enemy of the best. Spending time with Jesus is the best thing I can do. It's the one thing that is needed.

Our time belongs to Him.

There will be a price.

Let's pray: *Heavenly Father, today I will have decisions to make. These are decisions that may cause me to either draw closer or further from You. Help me to make spending time with You my priority. Help me to use the time You have given me wisely. There are things I believe I need to do today. Demands will also be made on my time today by others. You said that if I acknowledge You in all my ways You would direct my paths. (Proverbs 5:6) I am asking You to lead and guide me. I understand that there will be a price to choosing You. Anything worth having will require sacrifice. You said that the fear of man will prove to be a snare. (Proverbs 25:29) Help me to not be afraid or concerned about what others think in relation to my quest to be closer to You. Give me strength. Help me yield to the Holy Spirit, who is my guide and counselor, and not to my flesh. In Jesus' Name I pray – Amen.*

One Day at a Time

"When Enoch had lived 65 years, he became the father of Methuselah. And after he became the father of Methuselah, Enoch walked faithfully with God 300 years and had other sons and daughters. Altogether, Enoch lived a total of 365 years. Enoch walked faithfully with God; then he was no more, because God took him away." (Genesis 5:21–24 NIV)

Spiritual intimacy with God is developed over time, through consistency, in the community.

The genealogy listing noted in Genesis chapter five pauses to reflect on the legacy of a man named Enoch.

There's not a lot written in the Bible about Enoch, yet one statement speaks volumes about his life:

Enoch walked faithfully with God 300 years.

Let that sink in for a minute.

Other translations read:

"Enoch walked [in habitual fellowship] with God three hundred years after the birth of Methuselah ..." (Genesis 5:22 The Amplified Bible)

"After the birth of Methuselah, Enoch lived in close fellowship with God for another 300 years …" (Genesis 5:22 New Living Translation)

"Enoch walked steadily with God …" (Genesis 5:24 The Message)

I'm not sure what happened after he became the father of Methuselah. The Word does not record a specific circumstance that may have initiated this steadfast dedication.

What is clear is that Enoch lived to be 365 years old and he walked closely—*intimately*—with God for 300 of those years.

Three things are worth noting here:

1. **Spiritual intimacy with God takes time.**

    Recently, I was in an airport trying to get from one gate to another one which was much farther away. I had lots of time before my flight was scheduled to leave, so I decided to take my time and walk to the gate, instead of hopping the terminal train.

    The sights I saw walking along the long terminal were amazing. There were murals and designs on the ceiling and the walls of the airport that made me stop in awe. I saw elaborate pictures and videos of the city's famous history and stores I had not noticed when I was in the airport before. It was an amazing experience. I thanked God for nudging me to walk instead of ride. If I had not, I would have missed it all.

    When you walk, you see and experience things you wouldn't otherwise.

Walking is slower, but it is no less purposeful than other forms of movement.

Enoch walked with God.

When you walk with God, as you take time to be with Him, you will experience things you wouldn't have otherwise. You begin to see things as He sees them. It's not a quick process. Developing intimacy with God takes time. Which brings us to our second point:

2. **Spiritual intimacy with God is developed through consistency.**

A close friend worked for the public-school system for over thirty years. When she retired, she had a perfect attendance record.

Can you imagine going to work for over thirty years and never missing one day?

She never called in sick.

If the school doors were open, she was there.

Enoch walked with God 300 years. No one can touch that record!

Intimacy with God happens as we seek Him day by day. There are no Sunday-only meetings.

What would happen if you only communicated with the person closest to you once a week (if nothing else came up) for about sixty minutes (on average)? What would happen to that relationship *over time*?

We may spend less time with the Lord some days than others. That's normal and to be expected. The key is to make consistency the goal. Lastly:

3. **Spiritual intimacy with God <u>does not</u> require isolation.**

   Enoch was not a hermit.

   Besides Methuselah he had other sons and daughters. (There was a Mrs. Enoch somewhere!) Along with his family, Enoch had a thriving ministry as a prophet. (Jude 1:14–15) He lived a full life, yet God was at the forefront.

   You do not need to enter a monastery to be close to God. This will not require separating yourself from the world. The world needs believers in Christ who have been saturated in His presence!

   Scripture bears witness to this fact: the Christian life is to be lived out in the community. Enoch walked with God. He was on the move, with God. They talked and fellowshipped wherever Enoch went. He ministered to the people, with *God*. He took care of his wife and children, with God. God and Enoch did everything together!

   Hebrews 11:5 says, "Before his translation (Enoch) had this testimony, that he pleased God." I want to have that testimony and I believe you do too.

   There's an old joke that goes, "How do you eat an elephant?"

   The answer? "One bite at a time …"

How do we walk with God like Enoch did?

One day at a time ...

We need help to spend time with Jesus consistently. Let's pray:

Let's pray: Lord, my desire is to spend the rest of my life walking closely to You. I know being closer to You is Your will for me. Help me to be consistent in my walk with You. Lord, You know I have _____. (Fill in the blank. This may include a family, a person in your life that requires hands-on care, demands on your job or with your business, etc.) Let me not be negligent in the other areas You have called me to. Help me balance spending time with You and meeting my daily responsibilities. I believe You will show and teach me how to have a full life with You being primary. Help me to spend time in Your presence daily. I need You. In Your name Jesus, I pray, Amen.

God desires us to *walk* with Him. That means we are on the move, with Him. Don't leave God in the room after your prayer time. Talk with Him and fellowship with Him as you go about your daily duties. As we walk with God consistently, spending time with Him will be second nature for us. Walking with Him will be a routine part of our everyday life, like Enoch's was.

Our Daily Bread

"Give us this day our daily bread ..." (Matthew 6:11)

He will meet our need as we seek Him.

In the Old Testament, God gives the newly liberated Israelites instructions for gathering the manna that would be the staple of their diet for 40 years. (Exodus 16:4–5, 16–20) They are to:

1. Go out each day and gather the manna they needed according to the size of their family.
2. Not try to save manna from one day to the next. (Unless it was for the Sabbath day, any "extra" food would rot.)

Fast-forward to the New Testament.

The disciples ask Jesus: "teach us to pray." He tells them: "Pray for your 'daily bread.'" It's important that we ask God to provide for our needs and daily necessities: food, shelter, finances, etc. Yet there is a greater truth in this: just as the Israelites were required to gather manna each day to survive, spending time with God every day is necessary for us to survive and thrive!

Jesus is the bread of life. He is our *daily bread*. Jesus was teaching the disciples and us an important lesson. He was teaching us to focus on one day at a time, recognizing that each day has enough trouble of its own. (Matthew 6:34) He was teaching us to depend and focus on Him daily for everything we need.

We need more than the bills being paid and food on the table.
We need peace in our hearts when life has been turned upside down.
We need joy in the midst of pain.
We need to walk in His love when we would rather be unloving.

We can only get that type of bread in the presence of God!

I have spent time with God on one day and tried to live off that "bread" for days. You know what I have found? It doesn't work. Bread for Monday is for Monday. I have no idea what's in store for Tuesday, and if I don't spend time with Him Tuesday, I walk into the day blind, unprepared and undernourished! What happens by Friday if I haven't spent time with Him? Well by then *I stink!* My attitude is wrong, my direction is off and I'm hungry!

Another interesting thing happens when we seek to spend dedicated time with God daily. As we seek His face, He provides the other stuff we need from His hand. (Matthew 6:33)

I once heard a minister say that one of the saddest words is the word "tomorrow." How often do we put things off because, after all, we have tomorrow? God says today when you hear my voice, harden not your heart. (Hebrews 3:15) *I can imagine God saying, "When I whisper to you to spend time with me, don't put me off."* When we do that regularly over time, our heart grows a little colder. His voice becomes more and more faint.

"Lord, give me **this day**, my **daily** bread ..."

Spend time with the Lord today.

Let's pray: *Lord, I thank you for this time in Your presence. Minister to my spirit today. You know what this day holds. I don't. Give me the bread I need for today. Give me the wisdom, the joy, the peace, the discernment, the (fill in the blank) I need for today. Provide for my needs and thank you for allowing me to have some wants too. Thank you. In Jesus' Name I pray, Amen.*

Fear Not!

Exodus 20:18–21

"And all the people saw the thunderings, and the lightning, and the noise of the trumpet, and the mountain smoking: and when the people saw it, they removed, and stood afar off. And they said unto Moses, Speak thou with us, and we will hear, but let not God speak with us lest we die. And Moses said unto the people, Fear not ..." (Exodus 20:18–21)

Don't be afraid to draw close to God.

In this Old Testament passage, God descends in fire at Mount Sinai. There is thick smoke, thunder, lightning, and the mountain begins shaking. While they are in God's presence, the Israelites had been warned by Moses not to go up the mountain or to even touch its boundaries or they would die. It's all too much! The people are afraid. They stand far away ...

God desires a close relationship with us and continues even now revealing Himself to us. Like God's people did then, some Christians today choose to stand "afar off" from God. They may prefer to leave seeking God to other people—people they believe are more spiritual or more mature in the Lord. Spending time with God may feel like entering thick darkness ... It's scary. They may wonder if they are doing it right. They may feel unworthy. They may feel ashamed.

Although Moses had been in God's presence many times before, I wonder if he too was a little afraid at that moment. It was quite a scene. He wanted to be closer to God, though, so he drew near to the Lord.

"Draw nigh to God and He will draw nigh to you." (James 4:8)

It's important for every Christian to have their own personal relationship with God. When we don't spend time with God for ourselves, or if we don't believe God will minister directly to our hearts and minds, we will find ourselves depending on others to know what God is saying. We will go from one prayer and prophecy line to the next. We'll go from church to church and conference to conference to hear from the Lord. We become like the Israelites: "Speak thou with us, (Moses) and we will hear, but let not God speak with us …"

I was there for a period. Then, I began to feel a growing sense of discontentment within me. God revealed to me that I spent a lot of time and effort making plans and going places to hear *from Him*, but I didn't spend dedicated time *with Him* myself! Like the Israelites, I was content to let someone else tell me what I wanted to know from God. After this, I decided to put more emphasis on spending time personally in His presence. I needed to hear from Him directly. Attending a conference or special service would be a welcome supplement—not the main course!

There is a passage in Scripture that sends chills up my spine when I think about it. In 1 Kings 13:1–25, God tells a prophet not to eat or drink in a certain town, along with some other instructions. A second prophet (who lives in the forbidden town) tells the first one that God wants him to eat at his house. The first prophet does so. Then the second prophet tells the first prophet he will die for disobeying God's instruction and the first prophet is killed by a lion.

There is a lot in this story but the key for us today is this: we need to walk closely with the Lord so we hear and know God's direction for our lives. The Holy Spirit dispenses spiritual gifts within the Body of Christ (preaching, teaching, prophecy, etc.) to assist in the maturation and edification of the Body. We need other men and women of God to prophesy, teach, and minister to us and to reveal things to us that will help in our walk with the Lord. The issue comes when we substitute hearing from others for spending quality time with the King of Kings and Lord of Lords ourselves. We can't do what He says to do if we don't know what He says. If we have spent time with Him and have His guidance, it's less likely that we will detour in our obedience to Him—regardless of outside influences!

God has so much to say to us if we take time to go before Him and listen. Also, like Moses, when we press into God, He can better use us to help those that don't. I am extremely grateful for those that drew near to God themselves and then helped me in my walk with the Lord, before I understood the importance of being close to Him myself.

There is one more thing. God is love. He is faithful. He is also powerful and mighty! I can only imagine what the scene on Mount Sinai must have looked like, so it's no wonder the people were afraid. It's important that we have a *reverential* fear of Him. When we do, we won't take His commands lightly. "… For God has come in this way to test you, and so that your fear of Him will keep you from sinning." (Exodus 20:20b) God is holy and righteous. He is the same God now that He was on Mount Sinai!

God wants His people to come into His presence. We have a great High Priest, Jesus, who understands us! He says that we can boldly come into His presence to get the help we need. (Hebrews 4:14–16) This kind of boldness is not rooted in arrogance or pride, but with humility and with a surety that God cares and will answer our prayer!

It's important that we reverence God when we come into His presence. It is there that we find the help, the hope, the healing, the forgiveness, and the peace that we need.

Don't be afraid. He's waiting for you.

———

I thank God for all the people in my life that have helped me and are still helping me in my Christian walk. When I think about those people, one thing stands out: they all walk closely to the Lord. Their walk encourages me to seek the Lord more myself. That's what we should do for one another as Christians. Through our deeds and by what we say, we should encourage others to seek the Lord for themselves. God desires personal relationships with His children. He wants us to know Him for ourselves!

Don't be afraid to draw close to God. He desires closeness with us.

It's why He sent His Son Jesus to die. Our sins separated us from Him.

Draw near to God. He promises He will draw near to you.

Is Something Burning?

Exodus 3:1–4: "Now Moses kept the flock of Jethro his father in law, the priest of Midian: and he led the flock to the backside of the desert, and came to the mountain of God, even to Horeb. And the angel of the Lord appeared to him in a flame of fire out of the midst of a bush: and he looked, and behold, the bush burned with fire, and the bush was not consumed. And Moses said, I will now turn aside, and see this great sight, why the bush is not burnt."

Burning bushes are opportunities to draw close to the Lord.

Do you smell smoke? Is something burning in your life?

There are times when parts of our lives seem like they are out of control: our finances, our relationships, our career, our health. Sometimes it feels as if we have a four-alarm blaze on our hands!

What would you say if I told you God was in your fire?

That's what happened to Moses. He's going along, taking care of the sheep on the backside of the desert, like he always has for the past forty years, when suddenly he sees a burning bush. It's burning but it's not being destroyed by the flames. He turns aside to see what's going on and encounters God.

Burning bushes are opportunities to draw close to the Lord. They provide us with the chance to see God like we never have before.

What exactly is a burning bush? It's something out of the ordinary. It makes you catch your breath. It could be something you wouldn't wish on an enemy. Either way, God is extending an opportunity for you to get to know Him better in it ... through it.

Burning bushes come in the way of:

Unexpected layoffs

A sudden, unanticipated move

A new job assignment

An uncertain diagnosis

God often uses the circumstances in our lives to get our attention. He sure got Moses' attention.

Moses stopped to examine the burning bush closer. Scripture states that when the Lord saw that he turned aside to see, *then* God called out to him from the midst of the bush. "Moses, Moses!" He said. Moses replied, "Here am I" (Exodus 3:4).

The Lord told Moses to take his shoes off because the place he was standing on was holy ground. God then formally introduces Himself and Moses is given the assignment of a lifetime. (Exodus 3:5–10)

If we don't stop and turn aside, our burning bushes are just ... burning. There is something extraordinary that happens when we deliberately stop all other activity and take time to see what God is saying or doing in our situation. God notices when we stop. He speaks. It is a holy place indeed.

When we spend dedicated time in God's presence, we are turning aside.

Turning aside takes many forms. It happens when we unplug from our phones, the TV, and the computer for a while.

It happens when we fast.

It happens when we step away from people and the demands of the day, for a time, to pray.

It can be for a longer time or a short period. The key is, using that time, that space, to focus on the Lord. To be still in His presence.

Moses had to stop what he was doing and go out of his normal routine to examine the burning bush. It's the same for us. We can't just coast along and expect to see God along the way. At some point, we all should "turn aside." The thing is, it's easy to just go with the flow of life without taking time for Him. We don't do it on purpose, it just happens. Because God loves us, He'll keep reaching out to us.

What is God trying to tell you? What is He showing you?

He doesn't allow burning bushes for no reason.

What if Moses had not stopped what he was doing? What if he decided, "Nope, no time to stop. I'm too busy with these sheep today." Would he have missed God's call for his life and God's plan to free His people?

What do we miss when we don't spend that time with God?

When things happen in our lives that catch us off guard, it's simply an invitation to walk closer to Him than we have before.

Do you smell smoke?

Don't panic! This is your chance to know God as you have not known Him before. He is going to reveal Himself to you in greater dimensions than you have ever experienced. You will not be the same.

Turn aside.

Remember this: When things happen in our lives that catch us off guard, when surprises pop up, it's our invitation to know God better. It's an opportunity for our faith to grow stronger. It's a chance for God to be glorified through us! It may come disguised as trouble or as something very challenging. It may look like it will require more of us than we would care to give. Go before the Lord. Talk to Him about it. Ask Him to help you walk through it. Tell Him you want Him to be glorified in it. Tell Him you need Him to give you the corresponding strength, wisdom, and peace you need for every step of this journey. Listen to Him. He will guide you. Don't miss this opportunity.

You desire closeness with Him. This is part of the process.

Arise and Eat

"Arise and eat, for the journey is too much for you." (1 Kings 19:7)

When times are hard, draw close to God.

God displays the men and women of the Bible in all their moods and dispositions. In 1 Kings 19 we see the mighty prophet Elisha fleeing from Jezebel in the wilderness of Judah. He is alone and despondent. He prays that God might take his life.

It is indeed possible to call down fire from heaven one day, and to be in a dark corner with your head hanging low the next. Like Elijah, we say "I've had enough!" (1 Kings 19:4)

How does God respond to Elijah's plea? He tells him to "Arise and eat."

Why? Because "... the journey is too great for thee."

Mighty man or woman, in this life we will all experience situations and seasons that try us. We know God's promise is to never leave or forsake us, but the journey can be hard.

Before you reach the "I've had enough" point, follow these steps:

Stop. Don't keep up the "business as usual" façade. If you are hurting, admit you are hurting. If you are tired of a situation—say you are tired of it. The sooner you acknowledge where you are, the sooner you can come out of it.

Don't make any major decisions or plans when your mind is clouded, and your heart is heavy. The enemy has tricked people into doing unwise, hurtful, and sometimes permanent things to themselves and others in the midst of a temporary situation.

Get to a quiet place where you can be replenished physically. God did not scold Elijah for how he felt. He let him sleep and served him a meal. We are spiritual beings wrapped in flesh. It's important to recognize this. Not being strong physically will affect us spiritually. We should make getting the proper rest and eating nourishing foods a priority because this also affects our mental health and our overall Christian walk.

Finally, arise and eat. That is, spend dedicated time with God. Psalm 119:50 says, "This is my comfort in my affliction, that Your Word has revived me." Many of the psalms speak directly to dealing with hard times. Ask the Lord what you should read. God can lead you to Scripture that speaks directly to your issue. Allow Him to minister to you through His Word.

"Your words were found, and I ate them, and your words became to me a joy and the delight of my heart ..." (Jeremiah 15:16) Eat. Chew on His Word. Meditate on it. Digest it. Let His Word heal your heart and mind.

When you are beaten down, God will strengthen you. Tell Him everything. He says we are to cast (give or throw) all our cares on Him because He cares for us. (1 Peter 5:7)

Tell Him how you feel and what you think. Tell how you feel *about* what you think. Yes, He knows. But tell Him. Remember, He has called you to spiritual intimacy. He wants you to share your heart with Him so He can minister to you on a personal level.

Get a journal. Write it and release it.

Sometimes all you can do is sit. Sometimes you feel so numb you can't talk. Sit before God. Give Him time to speak to your heart. "Be still," He says, "and know that I am God." (Psalm 46:10)

God is the source of our strength. He's our joy. He's our peace. He is everything we need.

When the journey is too great for us, the enemy would love for us to lie down and give up!

Not so, says the Lord. We can "... live and declare the works of the Lord!" (Psalm 118:17)

There may be a time when you feel like you just can't do it alone or, after you have done all you know to do, you are still struggling. Ask for help! Call a trusted friend or a good counselor. Don't stop reaching out until you get the support you need. (See Ecclesiastes 4:9–12) Later in this passage, God tells Elijah to anoint Elisha as prophet. From that point on, Elijah had someone walking beside him on his journey. They were together until God called Elijah home. Having, needing, or wanting support does not mean you are weak. Admitting you need help in hard times is important. It's a key to the door of deliverance.

God can bring you out any way He chooses. Trust Him to do so. Trust His timing and His ways with you.

Arise, beloved child of God, and eat.

Hard times can reveal where we are in our relationship with Christ. We don't know what we are made of until the right pressure is applied.

Hard times can be a crossroads for people. Sometimes people can't handle it and they walk away from the only one who can really help. You may be frustrated, you may be confused, you may be angry. You might be angry with God. Don't walk away. You need Him now more than ever.

1. Stop.
2. Don't make any major decisions or plans.
3. Get to a quiet place where you can be replenished physically.
4. Spend dedicated time with God.
5. Get help when you need it.

Know this: God sees you. He will help you. He loves you.

Shut the Door

"When Elisha reached the house, behold, there was the boy lying dead on his couch. He went in, shut the door on the two of them and prayed to the Lord." (2 Kings 4:32–33)

Times of solitude are necessary when developing spiritual intimacy with Christ.

Often in Scripture, prayers for miracles were done in seclusion or away from the crowds. (Mark 5:35–42, 7:31–35, 8:22–25, Acts 9:36–41) The **spectators, scorners, or mourners** would be left outside while prayer to God took place in secret.

Jesus instructs us in Matthew 6:6, "But when you pray, go into your room, close the door and pray to your Father who is unseen. Then your Father, who sees what is done in secret, will reward you." There are times that we must find a place to get into the presence of God away from everything and everyone else. Even if the place we go to does not have a physical door, it needs to be a solitary place.

Why?

We are saying, in that act, "God, You are so important to me. Nothing else is important right now but You. I need You and You alone." The physical act of getting away shows how special and precious He is to us. We are not taking our relationship with Him for granted. We are saying, "Lord, You are worthy of my undivided attention!" When a husband and wife seek to spend intimate time together, they go into their bedroom, shut and lock the door. This says, we are not to be disturbed or interrupted. There are no spectators.

There are no spectators in our prayer closet with God either.

Solitude is necessary to shut out the scorners. Scorners don't believe in the power of God. Some may believe what you are praying for is beyond God's reach. They tell you to use common sense. Scorners may include thoughts of fear and unbelief that surface from within your own heart and mind.

Shut the door. Get completely alone with God. Declare: nothing is impossible with God (Luke 1:37), and God is able to do exceedingly, abundantly above all that I ask or think! (Ephesians 3:20) He is waiting for you to declare His Word. He watches over His Word with the sole purpose of doing as He promised! (Jeremiah 1:12)

When you are in solitude, you can't hear the cries of the mourners. The mourners have no hope. They say it's over. The mourners are so consumed with grief and despair that they cannot see what God can do in the situation.

In solitude, we close ourselves off from everything except God.

We are not focusing on the situation as it stands.

We are not focusing on how we feel.

When we focus on His might, His power, and His glory, mourning turns into praise!

Shut the door to unbelief. Shut the door to doubt and fear.

In prayer there are no limits except those that we self-impose.

Nothing is too hard for God!

Children are conceived when a husband and his wife are alone together, intimately. **Miracles are conceived** when we are alone with God in prayer!

Do you have a secret place for prayer? That is, a place where you can pray and be completely undisturbed? It's great if you have a room or closet you can go to, but if you don't that's okay. Ask the Lord to show you a good spot where you can be alone with Him. I read a story about a mighty woman of God with many children. When she wanted to pray, she would pull her apron up over her head to signify she was with God. Do what you have to!

Let's pray: *Lord, You said to "come apart and pray" (Mark 6:31). Help me to shut the door and pray to You in secret. Show me where to go and how to do it. Help me to focus on You and not on fears and unbelief, for You have not given me the spirit of fear, but of power, love, and a sound mind. (2 Timothy 1:7) I stand on Your Word that says, "with You, nothing is impossible." Nothing is too hard for You, God. You said if we could believe, we would see the glory of God. (John 11:40) More than anything I want to see Your glory in this situation. I ask for a miracle and yield and submit to Your perfect will. Thank you, Jesus. Thank you for being the great I AM. In Your name I pray, Amen.*

Divine Favor

"Then the king said unto me, For what dost thou make request? So I prayed to the God of heaven." **(Nehemiah 2:4)**

When you walk close to God, you are in a position to receive divine favor.

Nehemiah was the king's cupbearer. Kings in those days feared being poisoned by rivals wanting the throne. The cupbearer was required to sample the wine presented to the king before serving it to him. This position demanded closeness and trust. Because of his position to the king, he is invited to make a special request, which the king grants.

Queen Esther, because of her relationship to the king, is asked three times for her heart's petition. (See Esther 5:3,6 and 7:2.)

Because of the loving hospitality and care he received from the Shunammite woman, Elisha asks her, "What is to be done for thee?" (2 Kings 4:13).

God tells Solomon in 2 Chronicles 1:7, "Ask what I shall give you ..."

When these types of open-ended invitations are made in Scripture, they are generally done within the context of a close relationship. They demonstrate an awesome picture of how God will respond to those who truly love Him. "If ye abide in me, and my words abide in you, ye shall ask what ye will, and it shall be done for you." (John 15:7)

Notice the prerequisites: *"If you abide in me ..."* If we spend time with God on a regular basis.

"If my words abide in you ..." If we make His Word an active part of our everyday life by walking in obedience to it, then we can ask for what we will and it will be done for us.

Why?

Because when we do these things, we begin to know Him intimately. We know what God wants and doesn't want. We know what He likes and dislikes. We then ask for things in agreement with His desire and His will. If we are not close to Him, our requests can easily be self-centered and just plain carnal. "You ask and you don't receive, because you ask with wrong motives, that you may spend what you get on your pleasures." (James 4:3)

Read Mark 6:14–28.

The daughter of Herodias performed before King Herod at a party he gave for high-ranking officials of his court in Galilee. She must have given some type of performance, because "When she danced, it pleased King Herod and he hastily said, Ask of me whatsoever thou wilt, and I will give it to thee ..." Again, he vowed, "Whatever you ask I will give you, up to half of my kingdom." The dancing daughter then asked her mother, Herodias, what she should ask for. Herodias told her to ask for the head of John the Baptist on a platter. And she did just that.

The daughter and the king did not have a relationship based on closeness and trust. He enjoyed her dancing and he made a foolish oath in response to it.

The thing that amazes me is this: the king offered her anything she wanted—up to half his kingdom! Yet, she used this once-in-a-lifetime opportunity to carry out vengeance for her mother!

"And the king was deeply pained and grieved and exceedingly sorry but because of his oaths and his guests, he did not want to slight her (by breaking faith with her)." (Mark 6:26) John the Baptist was beheaded in prison. The executioner brought his head in a charger and gave it to the daughter, who gave it to her mother.

What happened to the daughter? We don't know. That's the last we hear of her in Scripture. We can bet she never got that kind of opportunity again.

One thing is true. When you know the heart of the King, you know what to ask for.

When we are not close to God, we cannot be trusted with that kind of open-ended favor!

Going back to our earlier examples, God's plan was for the wall and gates in Jerusalem to be rebuilt. God's plan became Nehemiah's plan. Through Esther's requests, the enemy's plan to kill God's people was stopped. Only as we spend time with our King do our prayers become the means by which God carries out His will on the earth.

Solomon was given wisdom to rule God's people (which was what God wanted) and so much more. The Shunammite woman simply had a heart of generosity and respect for the Man of God, with no strings attached. In turn she was blessed with a child. Like Solomon, God gave her what she hadn't even asked for.

There is nothing like experiencing the favor that occurs as a result of being close to God!

As you draw closer to the Lord every day, expect to walk in His favor.

When you seek His face, you will see His hand moving in your life.

Changed in His Presence

"Now when they saw the boldness and unfettered eloquence of Peter and John and perceived that they were unlearned and untrained in the schools (common men with no educational advantages), they marveled; and they recognized that they had been with Jesus." (Acts 4:13 AMP)

When we spend time with Jesus, we are changed to reflect His likeness.

When the Jewish religious leaders heard Peter and John speak, Scripture says they marveled. Peter and John were not taught in the finest schools as they had been. Where did their boldness, understanding, and wisdom come from? How is it they were able to explain religious truths so passionately yet accurately?

This was a direct result of walking with the Savior, being in His presence, asking questions and learning from Him consistently.

Jesus told Peter and Andrew, "Follow Me and I will make you fishers of men." As we walk closely with Jesus daily, He will make us what we naturally are not. How many times in Scripture did God change the names of individuals to match their changed character and the new identity that was developed during their walk with Him?

What is the prerequisite for change? Jesus says to us, "Follow Me."

As we walk closely to the Lord and spend time in His presence, we are changed.

Remember when Moses was on the mountain with God for 40 days and nights? Scripture states afterwards that his face shone. The people were afraid to come near him. Moses began to wear a veil on his face when he spoke to the people. (Exodus 34:28–33)

Moses was literally changed in the presence of God. When you and I spend time in His presence regularly, we are changed too! Our faces will shine spiritually and illuminate the joy and peace that comes from spending time with the Lord. Our thoughts change, our attitude changes, and the way we act changes. God transforms us into a new person by changing the way we think. (Romans 12:2) This change starts the moment we accept Jesus as Lord and Savior of our life. "… Anyone who belongs to Christ has become a new person. The old life is gone; a new life has begun!" (2 Corinthians 5:17)

As we are changed in His presence, people notice.

People you come across on your job and your daily routine will tell you their life story. They will ask you to pray for them. They want to know your thoughts on deeply personal matters. They are drawn to you.

Why?

Because you look smart? No! You are shining. The religious leaders understood that what they saw and heard in Peter and John had to be a direct result of walking with Jesus.

Some people may say, "You're a Christian, aren't you?"

Some people may not recognize what they are seeing at all. They just know that something is different about you.

Rest assured, it's not you or I that naturally has their attention, it's the Spirit of God in us that they are drawn to!

Matthew 5:16 states, "Let your light so shine before men, that they may see your good works, and glorify your Father which is in heaven." If you are a child of God, you don't have to make your light shine. You just need to "be." Let it shine!

Be yourself. Let the Christ within you be a part of your everyday life.

Some believers shout "Hallelujah, thank you, Jesus," at every turn! Every other sentence starts with "Praise the Lord!" That's fine. Just know that as you spend time with Him, walking with Him daily, your light gets brighter and brighter. People will be drawn to that light even without words.

There is a flip side to this too. Some people will run from you. They will go the other way when they see you coming. The same light that draws, also repels those who want to live in darkness. Light exposes. Some people aren't ready for the light of God to shine on their life. Some reject it.

John 3:20 and 21 state, "Everyone who does evil hates the light, and will not come into the light for fear that their deeds will be exposed. But whoever lives by the truth comes into the light, so that it may be seen plainly that what they have done has been done in the sight of God."

While some hate the light, others desire the light to reveal where they are in their walk with God. They want to change. They are grateful for encouragement and correction.

Only when we spend time with The Light can we see ourselves as we truly are. (See 1 John 1:5–10)

As we spend time with Him, we become what we naturally are not:

Faithful
Loving
Self-controlled
Full of peace and joy
Gentle

Others want that too.

We are changed in His presence.

_____

When people ask why you have peace or how you can smile and have joy during a difficult situation or comment on your demeanor, give the glory to God! Let them know that you could not behave in the manner you do or that you could not carry out your daily responsibilities without His presence in your life!

Brag on God!

I Will Give You Rest

"Come unto me, all ye that labor and are heavy laden, and I will give you rest." (Matthew 11:28)

Complete rest is found when we release the worries and concerns of our heart to God.

Recently I found myself upset about a situation that occurred during a relatively peaceful day. Because I had been so at peace prior to the situation, I disliked feeling all out of sorts. I needed help to quickly return to moving in peace and joy.

I prayed about the situation. I told God I didn't like feeling the way I did about it.

He spoke to my heart, letting me know that my peace did not need to be disturbed because of what happened and that I could continue in peace and joy through Him. I didn't have to retaliate or act funny, nor did I have to be upset on the inside.

With that, I made the choice to keep walking in peace.

Minutes later He spoke and said, "You have now released the situation to me so I can work."

My eyes teared up. It was amazing! I didn't have to fight or make my case or get all messed up. He had it! I could really move forward in peace and joy.

I could rest.

I know none of that would have happened had I not gone to Him with my feelings and thoughts.

Jesus says, "Come unto ME (emphasis mine) all ye that labor and are heavy laden, and I will give you rest."

When we talk to close friends or trusted confidants, we may feel better because we had the opportunity to vent. It's important to share our feelings with others who will listen and pray. They can help us sort out what is going on. They can help us put things in perspective.

Yet even then, we still may be fearful or anxious or unsure.

There are times, too, that people don't want to hear all our complaints and issues and moans and groans, even if they are legitimate. Sometimes they are dealing with their own issues and need us to be the sounding board for them.

Either way, **He promises if we come to Him, He will give us rest.**

As we lay our situation at His feet in prayer, God gives us rest from the inner turmoil deep inside us that affects our mind and emotions. Isn't that what we truly desire?

Hebrews 4:9 states, "… There is a full complete rest still waiting for the people of God." He is waiting for us to walk in peace and joy and rest. That is what He secured for us when He died for us.

The Scripture goes on to tell us to be careful because unbelief can keep us from entering that place.

Hebrews 4:15 and 16 remind us that we have a great high priest, Jesus, who understands what we go through and that we can come boldly to Him, to the throne of grace, in the time of need.

Spiritual intimacy with Jesus ushers in rest for our souls. True rest. This is not a light, "The sun will come out tomorrow! Chin up!" type of rest. This type of internal rest is undisturbed regardless of external circumstances. (See Philippians 4:6–7)

Jesus knows we are prone to labor and to be weighed down! We will try to work things out in our own finite strength. We carry our own burdens when we don't need to and pick up the burdens of others along the way.

We know He is God, but unbelief can creep in just like in the Garden of Eden.

"Has God said … ?" (Genesis 3:1)

Did He really mean it when He said He would never leave me or forsake me? Is God's Word true for me, in this impossible situation?

What is your "Has God said … ?"?

Go to Him with everything. He promises He will give you rest.

It's waiting for you—now!

When you are very close to a person, you tell them everything: the good, the bad, and the ugly. Only as we release all our concerns, worries, doubts, and fears to the Lord can we obtain the peace that surpasses all understanding. Yes, He already knows about them. But remember we are to cast our cares on Him. He wants us to bring everything on our hearts to Him so He can carry the load and we can rest. Nothing is too big or too small to tell Him about. If you don't feel His peace, there is more to release to Him. Let that be your guide. Keep pouring out to Him until His peace envelops you. Don't forget journaling too.

Jesus Satisfies

"... Whosoever drinketh of the water that I shall give him shall never thirst ..." (John 4:14a)

A relationship with Jesus Christ is the only thing that can satisfy our deepest need.

Snickers has a series of funny commercials promoting their product.

In the ads, the main characters are cranky and "not themselves" because they are hungry. The characters initially look like people other than who they really are. Once they eat the candy bar, their hunger is satisfied, and they become their actual selves in appearance. The tagline says, "Snickers satisfies."

I really like the commercials.

Jesus says, "I am the bread of life: he that cometh to me shall *never hunger*, and he that believeth on me shall *never thirst*." (John 6:35)

Psalm 23 says, "The Lord is my shepherd, *I shall not want*."

That sounds like *complete* satisfaction to me!

In John 4:5–30, Jesus meets a Samarian woman at a well. He tells her whoever drinks of the well water will be thirsty again, but if they drink of the water He gives, they will never thirst.

The woman is like "Amen! Lay it on me!" (my paraphrase).

Jesus asks the woman to call her husband.

You can imagine the thoughts in her head: *What? I thought we were talking about water, and what does He know about that!*

The woman replies she has no husband.

Jesus says, "You've got that right! You've had five husbands and the man you are with now is not your husband" (my paraphrase).

What's Jesus getting at?

The Samarian woman is thirsty, and she is looking for something to satisfy her thirst. We can't point fingers at her, though. Her issue is our issue too.

Everyone has needs they want fulfilled. Everyone has wants. Everyone is thirsty. What we *do* about it is the issue at hand. God placed spiritual thirst on the inside of each one of us, and earthly things can never fulfill spiritual needs! Never. Ever.

"O taste and see that the Lord is good ..." (Psalm 34:8) Jesus says: Try Me.

People and things will never and can never truly satisfy us. We will find ourselves disappointed by people if we look to them for that purpose. People will be disappointed with us if they look for us to do the same thing for them. People and things cannot make us complete. We will only accumulate more and more stuff or take on more and more projects or relationships or activities or whatever—in the search for satisfaction.

The Samaritan woman would say, "Amen, sister!"

Many thirsty people are frustrated. The joy and peace they desire is missing. They place unreasonable demands on those around them. They may have had many relationships, or many jobs, or many "somethings." They are constantly searching for what they hope will fulfill their needs.

Only Jesus can fill the emptiness in our soul.

Ever felt on edge and moody for no apparent reason? Have you ever felt like everyone and everything was getting on your nerves? Your reservoir is low. Like the characters in the commercials, you're hungry—*spiritually hungry*.

Jesus said, "Come to Me." Why? Because in His presence is fullness of joy! (Psalm 16:11) He promises to be a well of water in us springing up into everlasting life.

He can satisfy our thirst now and for all eternity. Nothing else can do that.

Sorry, Snickers. Jesus *truly* satisfies.

Let's pray: *Heavenly Father, Lord, I thank you for being all that I need and all I could ever want. You know me better than I know myself. You created me. Help me to not look to people and things for self-worth and satisfaction. Help me spend time with You regularly so You can fill me. Holy Spirit, thank You for being the constant supply of living water within me. Help me to rely on and trust in You for everything. May I never be thirsty for anything else but You. You are my Shepherd. I shall not want for anything. I shall not want another Shepherd. Thank you, Jesus! In Your name that I pray – Amen.*

It's Going to Rain

"And the rain descended, and the floods came, and the winds blew, and beat upon that house; and it fell not: for it was founded upon a rock." (Matthew 7:25)

Walking closely with God will not make us immune from the issues and problems of life.

I can clearly remember one morning, spending a glorious time with the Lord, basking in His presence and savoring His Word. It was a special time. I felt as if I had truly had a foretaste of heaven!

After that it was all downhill. The day went from great, to bad, to horrible in record time!

Later that evening I complained to God. "Why did you let this and that happen?" Translation: "I've been spending time with you. I did my part! Why didn't you hold up your end?"

I sounded like Martha after the death of Lazarus: "If you had been here, my brother had not died" (John 11:21). I thought we were friends, Jesus! *Where were you?*

God is good. He lovingly reminded me that being close to Him, in His presence, in prayer, in the Word, being a Christian, does not make me exempt from the issues of life.

Simply put, we will have problems in this life. Make no mistake about it. Anyone who tells you otherwise is not telling you the truth.

In Matthew 7:24–27, Jesus tells a story about two different types of people: those that hear His Word and obey and those that hear His Word and disobey. They are referred to as the wise and the foolish. Both groups have one thing in common:

The rain falls,

The floods come,

And the wind blows and beats on them.

In other words, they both go through problems.

The difference is, the wise—those that love the Lord, those that hear His word and obey Him—are still standing when it's all over. They may be bloody and bruised but God is still God in their situation. They may be struggling, but He is still the Lord and Savior of their life.

Even if it hurts.

Even if they don't understand why.

Walking close with God does not make us exempt from the issues of life. It does help us stand when life happens.

Remember Shadrach, Meshach, and Abednego. (Daniel 3:12–27) Loving God did not keep them *from* the fiery furnace. They were kept *in* it.

Seek God's face. Stay close to Him.

It's going to rain.

We are pressed on every side by troubles, but we are not crushed. We are perplexed, but not driven to despair. We are hunted down, but never abandoned by God. We get knocked down, but we are not destroyed. Through suffering, our bodies continue to share in the death of Jesus so that the life of Jesus may also be seen in our bodies. (2 Corinthians 2:8–10 New Living Bible)

Ride or Die

"And Ruth said, 'Intreat me not to leave thee, or to return from following after thee: for whither thou goest I will go …'" (Ruth 1:16)

A close walk with the Lord is developed as we are faithful to Him, even when it gets hard!

Have you ever had a friend that will stick with you no matter what?

Our human, often selfish hearts can be touched in such a way that we not only care for someone else, but we would give our all for them. Some people refer to this type of relationship as a friend who will "ride or die."

It's the person who has your back regardless of the situation. They go the extra mile with you time and time again. They have proven themselves in your life.

Think about Ruth.

Ruth's husband died. She was in a foreign county with her mother-in-law and sister-in-law Orpah, whose husbands had also died. There she was with no financial support, in a foreign land, in the middle of a famine. Her mother-in-law, Naomi, decides to go back to her homeland, where she has heard there is food. She tells her daughters-in-law that they should go back to their homelands as she has nothing to offer them.

They, however, want to go with her. "And they said unto her, Surely we will return with thee unto thy people." (Ruth 1:10)

Naomi then lays out all the reasons why they shouldn't stay with her, and by verse fifteen Orpah is headed home "to her people and to her gods."

Ruth, however, refuses to leave Naomi, and her plea is one of the most passionate in Scripture:

"But Ruth replied, 'Don't ask me to leave you and turn back. Wherever you go I will go; wherever you live, I will live, your people will be my people, and your God will be my God. Wherever you die, I will die, and there I will be buried. May the Lord punish me severely if I allow anything but death to separate us!'" (Ruth 1:16,17)

Whatever happens, I'm with you for life. Ride or die.

How does Naomi respond?

"When she (Naomi) saw that she (Ruth) was steadfastly minded to go with her, then she left speaking unto her." (Ruth 1:18) There was nothing Naomi could say. Ruth's mind was made up.

Faithfulness is the foundation on which intimacy is built.

Faithful says: "I will always be there. I'm not going anywhere." It is not dependent on circumstances but is fueled out of commitment and unconditional love.

Faithful does not say: "I am with you until …" Faithful says: "I am with you, period."

"Know therefore that the Lord thy God, He is God, the Faithful God, which keepeth covenant and mercy with them that love Him and keep His commandments to a thousand generations." (Deuteronomy 7:9)

"And I saw a heaven opened, and behold a white horse; and He that sat upon him was called Faithful and True …" (Revelation 19:11)

"While we were still sinners, Christ died for us." (Romans 5:8)

"Faithful" is the very nature of God. It's who He is! Sometimes, though, we are not faithful to God.

Spiritual intimacy will require us to keep walking closely to the Lord:

When we hurt
When we don't understand what He is doing
When what we have been praying for doesn't happen
When trouble seems to come by our home like an old friend
When we feel like giving up

It's easy to be faithful to someone when times are good. Spiritual intimacy requires us to walk closely to Jesus when the pain is so bad, we are tempted to walk away.

I knew a woman who lost two people, who were the closest to her, back to back. Their deaths were unexpected and sudden. She struggled with what happened. Where was God? Why did He allow this to happen? She stopped going to church and being in fellowship with other believers for a time. She needed to understand … why?

Situations like this are painful and hard. Like Orpah, some people decide (for a season or permanently) to go back to "their people and their (former) gods."

Ruth was faithful to Naomi when times were at their worst. She had to trust Naomi's instruction when it probably made no sense to her. Regardless of how things may have seemed, she stayed by Naomi's side. Naomi's God was her God in a desperate situation with seemingly no hope of change.

You can't be close to someone you don't trust. Do we trust Him?

Can He trust us?

Can He depend on us when life is hard?

Can He trust us with pain and disappointment and trials?

We need His help. We can't walk with the Lord this week, then disappear for a month. We need a steadfast mind to walk with God regardless of what the road looks like.

Nothing could deter Ruth or cause her to change direction.

After all they went through together, I believe one thing for sure: the relationship between Naomi and Ruth at the end of their story was a much stronger one than what they had at the beginning.

It's the same for us as we walk with God. When we go through life with Him, we love Him with a deeper love than before. "I'll never leave you or forsake you" is no longer one of many promises in His Word. (Deuteronomy 31:6) It's life itself.

If you haven't read Ruth's complete story, don't worry. She is more than blessed in the end. Ruth the Moabite is in Jesus' family tree.

———————

"... Hold fast to the Lord your God, as you have until now." (Joshua 23:8)

Lord, help me be faithful to You, through all the seasons of my life, as You are to me. In Jesus' Name I pray – Amen.

Overcharged

"Martha, Martha you are worried and upset about many things ..." (Luke 10:41)

When we are too busy, we risk being overcharged and less close to God.

Ever been there?

One morning I found myself in a doctor's exam room physically and mentally exhausted. It was the first time in a while that I had taken an extended moment to sit in silence. The moment was long enough to allow issue after issue to come running to the forefront of my mind.

"What brings you in today?" she asked. Something spilled out of my mouth and before I knew it, my physical became a counseling session. My physical state (as the exam revealed) was fine. My mental state, however, was another story.

Scripture describes it as being overcharged.

Jesus warns us in Luke 21:34, "Take heed to yourselves, lest at any time your hearts be overcharged with surfeiting and drunkenness and with the cares of this life ..."

Overcharged is defined in the Greek as to be weighed down or to be heavy. Jesus defines the root of the heaviness as surfeiting, drunkenness, and the cares or the anxieties of this life. The word *overcharged* speaks to overindulgence and excess. You may be quick to say, "Well, I don't get drunk or anything!" Okay. Have you ever had your heart weighed down to the point of excess by care and anxiety?

Life happens to everyone. Sometimes, though, concerns and fears about finances, loved ones, jobs and the like, can take an extraordinary toll on us mentally and physically. When our hearts are weighed down with worry or when we are just plain tired, it's easy to miss God. It's hard to hear Him speaking to our hearts. Focusing on His Word may be challenging. Concentrating during prayer may seem impossible.

Martha was "cumbered about much serving" (Luke 10:40). *Cumber* means to hamper or hinder, obstruct, to weigh down, burden, or encumber by being in the way. To be cumbered is to be distracted with care. It means to be driven about mentally. When a person is cumbered, they are over-occupied about a thing.

They are overcharged.

It doesn't matter what we are overly concerned or preoccupied with. Martha was not "in sin." Yet, we can find ourselves working so hard in the church, on our jobs, in our ministry, or in our homes that we miss Him altogether.

It can take a while before we realize the anointing—that is, the power of the Holy Spirit working in and through us—has been quenched. We become like Samson. We don't know our true state until the

Philistines of sin and carnality overtake us, and we are bound. We have no power. (Judges 16:1–21)

Like King Saul, we may still desperately try to keep up spiritual appearances before the people, though God's presence has long left us. (1 Samuel 15:10–31)

When we are in this place, every hill becomes a mountain and every valley is a lifeless wilderness. Fear, depression, anxiety, and unbelief roll in like waves. It's easy, like Martha, to be fed up with people—especially a family member who does not appear to be doing her fair share of the work.

In sports, when someone gets hurt or one team is unmercifully beating the other team, they call a time-out. This gives the hurting player time to get help. The losing team has time to stop, refocus, and get a new or revised plan. My doctor's visit was a mini, unplanned time-out. It forced me to stop and reevaluate where I was.

Jesus called time-out on Martha, telling her that she was the issue, not Mary.

"Take no thought for your life, what ye shall eat, or what ye shall drink, nor yet for your body, what ye shall put on ..." (Matthew 6:25)

Jesus says not to give our daily cares and concerns the primary place in our heart and mind. He is to have that place.

If you are overcharged today, spending some time alone with God is the first step.

Take a time-out!

I believe a major hindrance to spending time with God the way we want to is dealing with the cares of life! Our daily schedules and to-do lists are full of tasks and requests and needs and wants. If we don't monitor our day-to-day schedules closely, it's easy to fall off track in our pursuit of closeness to God! Next, our hearts become overwhelmed.

If you don't have any time to spend with the Lord, you are too busy.

If you don't have any time to nurture and be present for your family, you are too busy.

If you don't have time to get the proper rest … you get it, you are too busy.

What does your schedule look like this week? Aside from work or other responsibilities, have you carved out time for:

Family and friends time
Rest and relaxation
Physical activity
Recreational, fun activities

Along with being before the Lord daily, first, it's important to have balance in our lives. Look at your schedule and see what is missing. You may need to cut back on some things or eliminate them completely. There may be some things you should add that will be a benefit to you. Ask the Lord to help you create a schedule that promotes your spiritual, physical, and mental health. Pray about this as often as you need to—weekly or even daily. He will show you how to fine-tune your schedule, making the most important things primary.

"Before you call, He will answer, while you are yet speaking, He will hear!" (Isaiah 65:24)

"From the end of the earth will I cry unto thee, when my heart is overwhelmed: lead me to the rock that is higher than I." (Psalm 61:2) The Rock is Jesus.

Seeking for Jesus

John 6:24: "When the people therefore saw that Jesus was not there, neither his disciples, they also took shipping and came to Capernaum, seeking for Jesus."

It's important to have the right motives when we are seeking spiritual intimacy with God.

In John chapter 6 we see two distinct and powerful stories. In verses 1–13 Jesus feeds the multitudes with five barley loves and two small fish. Jesus then departs from the people. (John 6:15) Soon more people come, seeking Him. Why?

Jesus knows why. "Verily, verily, I say unto you, you seek me, not because ye saw the miracles, but because ye did eat of the loaves and were filled …" (John 6:26) Jesus says in essence, you seek me for carnal reasons: to have your flesh satisfied.

It's important as we seek to draw closer to the Lord that we seek Him for the right reasons and with the right heart. In his commentary on this verse, Matthew Henry states, "Many follow Christ for loaves and not for love." That's a true and sad statement!

God knows our motives. Darkness is like high noon to Him. Nothing is hidden from His sight. God does want us to bring our concerns and our cares to Him. He is our Father. The Word "father" means source. He wants to be our provider, our healer, our deliverer, and so on.

Sometimes it's hard not to come into His presence immediately reciting our to-do list. It's important, though, to hear what He has to say. We want to know His agenda. We desire to be made fit vessels to do His work.

We want to be careful not to make seeking Him for things the priority. We want to make Him the priority.

There are different groups of people mentioned in the gospels that had interactions with Jesus: the disciples and the multitudes.

Both groups of people are followers of Jesus, but there are distinct differences between the two.

The disciples have given up everything to follow Jesus. We are told they left behind careers and family members. Luke 5:11 says, "They forsook all and followed Him." They go where He goes and do what He does. (Matthew 10:1)

Scripture states that He spoke unto the multitude in parables, but when He was alone with the disciples, He expounded His sayings to them more clearly.

The multitudes appear in contrast to the disciples. They follow Jesus too, but from a greater distance. They may begin their walk as a disciple, but when Jesus declares things that are hard for them to comprehend, they leave Him.

Later in the book of John, Jesus preached, "Verily, verily, I say unto you, Except ye eat the flesh of the Son of man, and drink His blood, ye have no life in you …" (John 6:53). Some said, "This is a hard saying: who can hear it?" (John 6:60). Afterwards, "… many of his disciples went back, and walked no more with Him" (John 6:66).

Jesus has a way to separate those that truly love Him, the disciples, from the multitudes.

Scripture states that people who leave God were never with Him at all. (1 John 2:19)

The multitudes seek the Lord for loaves.
For signs.
When it is convenient.
When it requires nothing.

Jesus asked Peter, "Will ye also go away?" (John 6:67). Peter replies, "To whom shall we go? Thou hast the words of everlasting life. We believe and are sure that you are the living God!" (John 6:68, 69)

When God asks something from you that you may not understand, or something you do not like, or something you would rather not do—how will you respond?

The amazing thing the multitudes don't understand is this: it's impossible to seek His face and not have His hand!

"Seek ye first the Kingdom of God and His righteousness and all these *things* shall be added unto you …" (Matthew 6:33) When we make Him our hearts desire, He can give us the desires of our heart because our heart is lined up with His.

Are you a disciple or part of the multitude?

In the 33rd chapter of Exodus, God declares that He will bring His people into the Promised Land, but He will not go with them. The people have been rebellious and the Lord states, if He goes with them, He might destroy them on the way! Their passage into the land, however, will be secured, for He will send an angel before them to drive out the pagan nations, their enemies, from the land.

Later, Moses talks with the Lord. Moses said to him, *"If your Presence does not go with us, do not send us up from here."* He continues, "How will anyone know that You are pleased with me and with Your people unless You go with us? What else will distinguish me and Your people from all the other people on the face of the earth?"

Moses says, there is something we need more than the blessing. Lord, we want YOU. We want and we need Your presence. Moses is saying, in effect, I know what my one thing is. It's You, Lord. Nothing else matters. I am—we are—nothing without You.

This attitude of heart does not come naturally. We must pray and ask God to give us this kind of heart.

There was a period when I found myself not spending focused time with God. My attitude towards being with Him had gotten passive and casual. When I noticed it, I couldn't understand why I felt that way. I wasn't in active sin (I thought). What was it?

The Holy Spirit showed me that I had been praying for something urgently that had not come to pass. In response, I stopped making Him my priority. I had, in fact, been seeking Him for loaves. Because He hadn't answered my prayer in the manner I desired, my push to spend time with Him cooled. At that time, my primary motive for seeking Him was wrong.

I wasn't sure when this change of heart occurred, but somewhere along the line my desires outranked being in His presence. It happened subtly. I repented. I must ask God to reveal hidden motives in my heart and to cleanse my heart on a regular basis.

My desire is to be a disciple. I want to be a follower of Christ and Christ alone.

What is your desire? Are you seeking Him for loaves or for love?

How much time do you spend just worshipping God?

Nothing will bring us closer to the heart of God than worship.

When we worship God, we take our eyes off ourselves, off our situations, and we focus on Him. He becomes magnified.

It's important that God hears from our lips how important He is to us.

When a man and woman are dating, they often spend time telling each other how much they care for one another. They complement each other regularly. They are quick to say "thank you" and "I love you." This spills over into the honeymoon period. After a couple has been married for a while, they may not do this often. It becomes easier to take the other person for granted. We don't want to let that happen in our relationship with God. He needs to know we love Him—without strings attached. Whether He blesses us the way we want Him to, or not. Whether He answers our prayers according to our wishes, or not.

Regular worship of the Lord helps remind us why we should serve and love Him. It helps keep our heart clean and our motives in check.

Do we seek Him for loaves … or for love?

It is easier to have misplaced motives when seeking the Lord than you may believe. Jeremiah 17:9 states, "The heart is deceitful above all things, and desperately wicked: who can know it?" We can easily be deceived about the true state of our heart if we are not on guard.

How can we be sure we are seeking God with pure motives? Pray! Using the Scriptures below (and any others the Holy Spirit directs you to), ask the Lord to reveal any hidden motives and to give you a clean heart.

"Search me, God, and know my heart: try me, and know my thoughts: See if there is any offensive way in me and lead me in the way everlasting." (Psalm 139:23–24)

"Create in me a clean heart, O God; and renew a right spirit within me." (Psalm 51:10)

Don't Hide

"And he said, I heard thy voice in the garden, and I was afraid, because I was naked; and I hid myself." (Genesis 3:10)

Sin often causes us to hide from God.

Sin exposes us. It makes us see ourselves as we truly are in the flesh: weak, vulnerable, and in desperate need of a Savior. Unfortunately, that realization often causes us to run away from the very one who can change our condition.

God walked and talked with Adam and Eve. They shared intimacy with God as no other humans would. Sin caused them to hide then and sin causes us to hide now.

Sin disrupts spiritual intimacy. It makes us run away when He calls, "Where are you?" His presence, our delight and comfort in the past, is now something we dread. Yet it's now, more than ever, that we should run to Him with all our might.

The prodigal son came to himself and went home. (Luke 15:11–32) He understood full well the weight of all He had done, but he knew there was nowhere else to go. He needed help from his father.

We need the help of our heavenly Father when we sin.

I am amazed when I read of all the times (back to back to back) that the Israelites messed up. Yet the Word says, when they cried out to the Lord, He answered their cry.

Have you ever had a fatted calf experience like the prodigal son? I have and it's overwhelming. When you know how bad you have messed up, you simply want to walk behind the house and sit in the dirt. You dare not raise your head or attempt going in the house.

When the Father prepares a banquet for you, when He puts a ring on your finger, when He still takes care of you and blesses you beyond anything you could have ever imagined **after** what you did, **after** you shamed Him, it's really more than the heart can stand and the mind can comprehend.

His love knows no bounds.

Don't hide.

Tell Him how you messed up. You sinned. You were wrong. He is right.

There is a movie line that goes, "Love means never having to say you are sorry" (from the 1970 film *Love Story*). That's not true. As we seek to love God more and grow closer to Him, we have to say we are sorry when we sin. We've got to repent. We must do things His way. There can be no making excuses.

You may be ashamed and embarrassed. You may wonder how you could have ever ended up in the place you are in now. Don't run away from the Lord; run to Him.

He sees you, even if you are a great way off.

Come home.

———

"If we confess our sins, He is faithful and just to forgive our sins, and to cleanse us from all unrighteousness." (1 John 1:9)

"The LORD is compassionate and merciful, slow to get angry and filled with unfailing love." (Psalm 103:8)

"The LORD remains near to all who call out to Him, to everyone who calls out to Him sincerely." (Psalm 145:18)

"… I have loved you with an everlasting love …" (Jeremiah 31:3)

Loving People, Loving Him

"A new command I give you: Love one another. As I have loved you, so you must love one another." (John 13:34)

Loving others is part of loving God.

Have you ever been angry with someone who has wronged or mistreated you openly? What if they have behaved badly towards you over a long period of time, consistently? Do you pray for your enemies and do good to them, as the Word commands? Do you pray that they come to know the Lord (if they are not saved), or that they would walk in His love and righteousness if they are a believer? Do you ask Him to reveal anything you might have done in the situation to cause or add to the strife? Do you ask the Lord to mend the relationship, if possible?

When you are in this type of situation you may find yourself doing all these things, some of them, or none of them. It's hard when thinking about a person makes you feel a slow burn on the inside. If you hear about something unfortunate happening to the person or people, you may want to break into a happy victory dance. Most people have been here at one time or another in their lives.

I was in this place some time ago, when God dropped this Scripture in my spirit: "If a man say, I love God, and hateth his brother, he is a liar; for he that loveth not his brother whom he hath seen, how can he love God whom he hath not seen?" (1 John 4:20)

Did I hate the person? I can positively say I did not love or like them at all. I can also say just thinking about them made me very, very angry. I was also desiring spiritual intimacy with God. I could not seek to love God and despise the person at the same time. I have heard people say, "I love God; I just don't love people." Nope. That won't work.

Through much prayer and by the power of the Holy Spirit, over time, I forgave the person. I released them from the penalty I wanted them to pay for the offense.

I let it go.

"And this **commandment** (emphasis mine) we have from him. That he who loveth God, love his brother also." (1 John 4:21) We will dislike things people do and say. We are not free, however, to walk in hatred and unforgiveness toward them because of it. Hatred towards my brother takes me away from God. Unforgiveness causes my prayers to be ineffective and null. I can't walk in unforgiveness and walk in right relationship with God too. (Matthew 5:22–24, 6:14–15, Psalm 66:18)

Guess what?

That would not be the last time someone would make me very angry. I discovered that I could be easily offended and would hold on to my hurt feelings long after the offense occurred.

I realized my pursuit of a close walk with the Lord would be easily halted if I chose to take each issue to heart and to walk in anger, hurt, fear, and unforgiveness every time the opportunity arose.

The fact is we have many chances to walk in unforgiveness and strife in this life. People will say and do things to us we won't like, and unfortunately, we have the same capacity to say and do things to others they don't like. In order to walk in spiritual intimacy with God, it's important that we prepare ourselves to walk in love and forgiveness with others before the offense even occurs while watching our own walk, so we don't intentionally offend others.

When even minor things come up now, I find myself hurrying to set things right and forgive or to ask for forgiveness so I can move on in peace with the person and with God.

Whatever happened or happens, it's not worth your walk with the Lord.

Let it go.

Give it to God.

_____

To prepare:

Read: Matthew 18:21–35.

1. Know that people will do things that will hurt you and make you angry.
2. Know you can do the same things, even if it's unintentional.
3. Remember that as a Christian, your sin debt (which was beyond enormous) has been paid. (If you are not a Christian, provision has been made to pay your enormous sin debt too. You just need to accept it.)

4. Release others as you have been released! (Freely and as quickly as possible!) Ask God to help you with this.
5. Know that only as you release others can you walk in the freedom forgiveness gives. (Freedom from the bondage of bitterness, anger, and strife in your own spirit.)
6. Trust God to handle the situation. He sees it from all sides. He is a just judge.

Starting Over

"Nevertheless, I have somewhat against thee, because thou hast left thy first love. Remember therefore from whence thou art fallen and repent and do the first works ..." (Revelation 2:4–5)

This is where to start when He is no longer first in your life.

In His letter to the church of Ephesus, Jesus commends them for all they have done for the sake of the kingdom:

"I know thy works and thy labor and thy patience, and how thou canst not bear them which are evil; and thou hast tried them which say they are apostles and are not and hast found them liars: and hast borne, and hast patience, and for my name's sake hast labored, and hast not fainted. **Nevertheless** *..."* (Revelation 2:2-4)

Nevertheless?

Not the word you would expect after such a list of commendations. Despite all they have done and accomplished, they are found lacking.

Their love relationship with the Lord had changed.

It's frightening to think you can do a lot <u>for</u> the Lord and not be in love <u>with</u> the Lord.

Much like the distant married couple that remains together for the kids, they were Christians in name, but somewhere along the way their love for Christ became cold, sterile, and mechanical. He is no longer first ...

Solomon comes to mind.

When you read about the life of Solomon in 1 Kings, his relationship with the Lord is so exciting. Solomon lives to do the will of his Lord out of His love for the Lord. God blesses him with extraordinary wisdom. What could go wrong? 1 Kings 11:1 states, "But King Solomon loved many strange women ..." What happened next? "... Solomon <u>went after</u> Ashtoreth the goddess of the Zidonians and <u>after</u> Milcom the abomination of the Ammonites." (1 Kings 11:5) Other relationships occupied the place God was meant to have in his heart. 1 Kings 11:4 states, "For it came to pass after Solomon was old that his wives turned away his heart after other gods ..."

Know this: an increasingly growing love for God is not automatic.

For any relationship to work there must be effort put in. Relationships between people die because someone or both parties have simply stopped caring enough to put any effort into it. Jesus says, "I'll never leave or forsake you." He is always there for us. We, with our modern-day idols, are the ones who back away.

It doesn't happen overnight. It's a gradual process that sort of sneaks up on you. I think the slow and gradual route of sin is a great trick of the enemy. It's easy to call out the blunt, in-your-face, radical sin. The enemy's best tool is to encourage us to back up from our relationship with God a little here, a little there.

You don't have to pray right now.

Read the Bible later.

Don't worry about church, you can go next Sunday.

What's wrong? Other people are doing it. One time won't hurt.

Solomon confirms that starting out well won't guarantee we will finish well. Our relationship with Christ takes effort. We are saved by grace and not works—that is, by who we believe in and not what we do. Yet, we are admonished to "work out our own salvation with fear and trembling" (Philippians 2:12).

Protect and cultivate your relationship with the Savior, at all costs.

When we don't serve God out of love, we serve Him out of obligation. Then we don't seek to serve Him at all.

If the wisest man in the world could make this mistake, who are we to think it could not happen to us?

Now what?

Maybe at one point you were on fire for the Lord. Now things have cooled. Going to church is what you are expected to do. Prayer is what you are supposed to do. Anything else is extra and who has the time?

No one close to you has said anything or seems to notice, but in your heart, you know.

The remedy for this condition of the heart is in verse 5.

First, **remember**. Go back to the early days of your relationship with the Lord. You prayed with childlike faith and saw answers beyond your wildest dreams. Just talking with Him and being with Him thrilled your heart. The Word was so exciting; so many revelations, Scriptures popped off the page, just for you. During praise and worship, who needed music? You could make up songs and sing to Him forever. You couldn't wait to be alone with Him.

Take the time. Remember.

Then, **repent**. Admit you are no longer there. It's your issue and no one else is to blame. You may have gotten here because of negative things that happened in your life (I willfully sinned and walked away from God) or positive (I got a promotion and started working longer hours, which meant less time for my normal devotion with Him).

The enemy of our souls does not care much about the means of our separation from God.

You must take responsibility for it, though. It is sin. Let God know you are sorry for neglecting your relationship with Him.

Do the first works. What did you do when you were really growing closer to the Lord? But, you say, I have children and a spouse now! The ministry is taking off! Or, things are at their worst and I'm so busy. I just don't have time. I just can't.

But you can.

Spend uninterrupted time with Him right away. Don't put it off. Make the effort, make the sacrifice.

Do it today.

Start with talking to God. Set an alarm or make an appointment on your calendar to meet with God every day. Even if you meet with Him for 10 to 15 minutes, start there. Ask God to help you. You may be in a different place or season of your life now. He knows that. Ask Him how to make your relationship with Him your priority every day, where you are now. God will show you the adjustments to make in your walk with Him as you go.

Tell another mature brother or sister-in-Christ that you trust where you are. You need someone you can be accountable to. James 5:16 states, "Confess your sins to each another, and pray for each another, that ye may be healed. The earnest prayer of a righteous person has great power and produces wonderful results." This will help in your deliverance and the person can be interceding for you. Ask them to check on you to see how you are doing regularly.

Let's pray: *Lord, forgive me for how I have been treating You. I have ignored our relationship/not spent time with You/not been faithful to You. I have allowed other things to take priority in my life. You are no longer my first love. I want this to change. Show me the idols in my heart and help me remove them. Help me put the things in my life in their proper place. I want to love You with all my mind, heart, and soul. I truly want to put You first but I'm not sure how to do this. I need help. Show me how to make You my priority every day. Help me, Holy Spirit, to be obedient to Your direction and guidance. Thank You for being faithful to me. Make me faithful to You. Amen.*

Follow Me

"… Follow thou Me." (John 21:22b)

God will direct us when it comes to spending time with Him. *Let God lead!*

This story as portrayed in Scripture makes me smile. Jesus had just told Peter how he would glorify God through his death. Peter, in turn, sees John and asks basically, "What's going to happen to him?" Jesus replies, "If I will that he tarry till I come, what is that to thee? Follow thou Me." Basically, He says, "It's really none of your concern, Peter, you just focus on Me." The disciples take Jesus' statement to mean John would not die! This is totally how we act! Sometimes we can be overly concerned about what God is doing in the lives of others. We compare what He is doing in their life with ours.

I have found that to be true when it comes to pursuing spiritual intimacy with God. There are a few things worth noting:

1. We can find many places in Scripture when Jesus departs to a solitary place to spend time with His Father. We read how He gets up to pray before the crowds come. As we follow Him, we will do the same. We'll make sure we have times of solitude in His presence.

2. Jesus told Peter (paraphrase), "Don't worry about my journey for John, you follow Me." What draws others closer to God may not be the same for you. For example, I like to sit, read, pray, and be silent for a while in God's presence. My husband likes to walk while praying and listening to the Lord. Some people listen to music to set an atmosphere of praise and worship as they spend time with Him. Some spend time with Him early in the morning. Some, at intervals during the day. Still others seek His face at night when everything is still. There are those who will sit in His presence for hours at a time. Some can only get away to be with Him for a small amount of time here and there. That's okay. We're not called to follow each other. We are called to follow Him! If each of us will listen to Him and see where He guides us, we will find our unique places where we are closest to Him.

3. As in any vibrant relationship, God likes to mix it up a little. He will call us to spend time with Him when and where we least expect it.

   I remember two instances that stand out clearly in my mind. In the first, I wanted to spend time with the Lord before I went home. I drove behind my job to a grassy area with a park bench. There was a large, scraggly tree hanging low near the bench. The area was rough looking. There were branches and leaves and stuff everywhere. The table was worn and dirty. It looked like the area had not been maintained in a while. It was not my usual type of spot. I cleared off a space and sat down with my Bible and notebook. As I sat down, the wind whistled through the leaves of the branches. It was so peaceful. I just sat there for a while, not reading or formally praying. I thanked the Lord for being in His presence. He then began to speak to me so much that at one point I just started crying. I felt like I was in a spiritual downpour!

It was as if He had been waiting on me to finally settle down so He could say what was on His heart. It was an amazing time with Him.

Another time after that, I was out of town at a conference for work. During a meeting break, I sat on the hotel patio outside the room to get some fresh air and some sunlight. Other conference participants and hotel guests were on the patio as well. As I was sitting there, I could sense the Holy Spirit inviting me to spend time with Him. *"Here? Now?"* I thought. The people were loud, drinking, smoking, and carrying on. Nope, this was not the place to spend time with God. Yet the tug was heavy on my heart to sit there and fellowship with Him ... which I did for a little while. I just couldn't get past the atmosphere. I thought to myself, when I go to my hotel room it will be nice and quiet and peaceful. We can talk then. What happened later when I got to my room? You may have guessed it. I didn't sense His presence the way I had earlier. I was following my own ideas and my own thoughts about how (and where) time with Him should be. I was not following Him.

Spiritual intimacy is achieved when we yield to Him to determine what works in our lives, instead of trying to follow a formula or do stuff like other people. The way intimacy with God looks is different for different people and may differ in our lives from year to year, week to week, or day to day.

Spiritual intimacy with God is special and private. Don't be overly concerned about what others are doing when they spend time with God. While there are basic things to do when you are spending time with God (prayer, worship, Bible reading and meditation, listening, etc.), be open to the leading of the Holy Spirit as far as what to do, when, and where each time.

Follow the Lord.

———————

Scripture states that Jesus got up before daylight to spend time with the Lord. I think it is important to talk to the Lord at the beginning of your day, whenever that is. That sets the tone for the rest of your day. It helps focus your mind on Him before life happens! To be honest, when I start my day, I prefer to talk to Him before I talk to anyone else (even my family!). That doesn't always happen, but it's a goal. Some people like to spend time with the Lord early because that is when they have the least distractions and can fully focus on God. Some people aren't fully alert until later in the day. Some prefer to spend time with the Lord in the evening or at night when their day is complete, and they can be still before Him.

The key is to get some time in and to be willing to sacrifice to do it! God will lead you if you ask Him to.

"My sheep listen to My voice; I know them, and they follow Me." (John 10:27)

Seasons Change

"To everything there is a season ..." (Ecclesiastes 3:1a)

Time with God may look differently depending on what season of life we are in.

Seasons in life change. The way you are close to the Lord in one season may totally change the next season.

I remember having a special spot in my home where I would meet with God for hours to pray and talk and read His word.

I had a spare bedroom in my home that served as my place for prayer and fellowship with God. I could shut the door and spend time with Him, undisturbed, for hours on end. There were windows in the room that allowed me to see the beautiful trees outside the house. I would reflect on His goodness and bask in the sunlight shining through the windowpanes. It was my sanctuary.

Then, someone needed to live in my home. Guess what room they moved into?

Right! OUR room.

I was thrown off. No other place seemed to be as good.

Then I found a great spot on my porch to meet with God. The porch was a great place to meet with Him early in the morning, with spring breezes blowing and birds singing His praises. Then the weather got cold.

I pouted. The season had changed.

In earlier years, I would spend hours of uninterrupted time with the Lord. It was great! When I had a family, uninterrupted time was more of a luxury.

Season's change in nature. Season's change in life.

My desire to spend time with God had not changed, so I was frustrated. I struggled to meet with Him because I was trying to do the same things I had done before. I struggled for a while too.

I don't know when it happened, but it did. It occurred to me that God knew all about the room, my responsibilities, my schedule—my life. I might not have been able to sing the Alleluia chorus to Him in our room with the sun beaming on my face for hours, but I could spend thirty minutes in His presence alone in the bathroom. Or 20 minutes in the car. Or 10 minutes on the patio.

The Lord gave me a job where I would travel periodically. I could have extended, uninterrupted time with Him alone! Hallelujah!

Season's change!

During my times of struggle, I don't remember saying, "God, closeness between us may look different or be in a different place. Can you please guide and lead me to the places/times for us?" I mourned (and pouted) too often and too long. I am learning now to follow Him. He wakes me up early a lot, and often I find I am alert and ready to hear from and be with Him. Sometimes He tells me to come away in the middle of the workday for my break. Sometimes He speaks in the late hours when the house is quiet.

Sometimes He just wants Me to be quiet and still before Him. It's important that I don't try to just push past that and study. Sometimes He just wants me to worship. Sometimes He wants to spend *extended time* teaching me principles from His Word. He's teaching and showing me more and more how to tune in to Him consistently; each day, every day.

We don't wear shorts during the winter months (at least we don't in the Midwest!). We don't wear a snowsuit when it's 90 degrees outside. We change our clothing accordingly when the seasons change, without much thought. When seasons change in our walk with the Lord, when He desires something else or something different; it's important that we change what we are doing and are not tied to doing things like we've always done them. Sometimes we don't realize the season has changed because it has happened gradually. It's important to ask God to help us become aware of when He is trying to shift things in our lives. We need to ask Him to help us stay in tune with Him.

Remember, seasons change.

There are seasons when we can spend extended time with the Lord regularly. Take advantage of these seasons. From those times, we have a flowing well to draw from when we need it later, when we can't spend as much extended time with Him.

Don't think shorter times of fellowship are less meaningful. God can minister to us powerfully here. We can worship Him, pour out to Him and be strengthened in our inner man in short times too.

Purposefully focus on tuning in to Him all day. Prayer at the beginning of our day helps us be more mindful of Him all day long.

In the House

"I was glad when they said unto me, 'Let us go into the house of the Lord.'" (Psalm 122:1)

Regular fellowship with the Body of Christ promotes spiritual intimacy with God.

I believe that some people equate spiritual intimacy with God with church attendance. Sometimes, churches have programs on top of programs and the thought seems to be the more you love Jesus, the more programs you will attend.

Church attendance and spiritual intimacy with God are two distinctly separate things, yet they enhance one another.

Spiritual intimacy with God is developed in private, behind closed doors. It's the relationship you have with God when no one else is around. It consists of your private prayer time, personal devotional time, worship, fasting, Bible study, and meditation on His Word. It consists of your regular giving to God's work. When we attend our local church assemblies, we experience our relationship with God in community. We pray together, worship together, study God's Word together, fast together, give together, etc.

As we fellowship, it should increase our desire to spend time with God outside of church. I believe that is one of the primary signs of a healthy church.

Consequently, as we spend time with God on a personal level, we should desire more to be an active part of a body of believers. It is there that we can share what God is doing in our lives. We can share the experiences of others who are also seeking spiritual intimacy with God. We are strengthened when we spend time with others who love God. They help bear our burdens. We help bear theirs. We all learn how to truly love God.

One key to experiencing closeness with God is by being part of a healthy, strong, Christ-centered church community.

In order to be a healthy member of a church community, we need to have a personal, close relationship with God.

I have come across many Christians who are not active members of any body of believers. Nothing really prevents them from being part of a church fellowship. They simply choose not to be. Or, they have joined a local assembly of believers, but don't participate in services on a regular basis.

God's Word states, "Let us hold fast the confession of our faith without wavering; (for He is faithful that promised) and let us consider one another to provoke unto love and to good works: Not forsaking the assembling of ourselves together, as the manner of some is; but exhorting one another; and so much the more, as ye see the day approaching" (Hebrews 10:23–25).

When we come to church, we encourage each other to seek closeness to God on a personal level. We help each other grow. Coming to church, though, cannot substitute for our own personal closeness with God. We will never grow in the Body of Christ and experience all that we can as a member of a local church family, if we don't cultivate our own personal relationship with Him.

Two people can attend the same church. One person can grow and get so much out of service, while the other will not. Why? One answer lies in each person's personal devotion to Christ outside the church walls.

Regular church attendance at a strong, Bible-based, Christ-centered church will cause you to seek to be closer to God personally. Seeking to be closer to God personally will cause you to desire being an active part of a local body of believers. Again, the two are interrelated.

There are people in places or situations where they simply cannot be a part of a local body of believers. There are exceptions. In general, followers of Christ need to be around other followers of Christ.

We need God.

We need each other.

Are you part of a local body of believers? If so, great! Your times of closeness with the Lord will help you grow spiritually so you can help others. God can use your gifts to benefit the entire body.

If you are not part of a local body, why not? Are you looking for a church home now? If your schedule or present circumstance does not allow regular attendance with a church or ministry, what are some ways you can still fellowship with other believers? Pray about everything. The local Body of Christ needs you.

Say Yes!

"Jesus replied, 'All who love me will do what I say. My Father will love them, and we will come and make our home with each of them.'" (John 14:23)

Disobedience hinders our relationship with the Lord.

Full confession. I can't tell you the number of times I have started a sentence with, "I'm not doing …" whatever is being asked of me. My first response to many requests, in general, is "no." Whenever an opportunity is presented to me, I see the hills and hurtles front and center. Oh sure, it will be awesome in the end, but that's down the road of the journey. I'll sit this one out, thank you!

This is a big issue in my life that I never fully realized until recently. I'm happy to say that the Lord is helping me say "yes" more often, and I am enjoying life and enjoying doing things that challenge me—things I previously steered clear of.

My saying "no" also spilled over to my walk with the Lord. I have been disobedient to Him more times than I care to admit. My responses to things He asked me to do have ranged from simply not doing it to putting it off for as long as possible. Right now, I am teaching a class about Jonah. He was a prophet in Scripture who was blatantly disobedient to God. I know this man Jonah for I am him at times: stubborn, childish, and self-absorbed. As God was merciful with Jonah, He has been merciful to me.

I am reminded of the time when God commands Abraham to sacrifice Isaac, his only son. (Genesis 22:1–19) Scripture reads, "So Abraham rose early in the morning …" to do what God required. Scripture does not say that he wrestled with God about it, that he discussed it with Sarah, or that he made plans to do it the following week. He moved immediately.

In Genesis 6 verses 13–21, God commands Noah to build an ark. The instructions are mind shattering. Verse 22 states, "Noah did this; he did **all** (emphasis mine) that God commanded him."

In the book of Exodus, God gives Moses commandments for the building of the tabernacle and the furnishings and the ordination of the priests and their clothing. The extremely detailed instructions go on and on for pages in Scripture. Moses does as the Lord commanded him.

In John 5:30b, Jesus said, "… I seek not mine own will, but the will of the Father which has sent me." He also said, "My food is to do the will of Him who sent me and to finish His work" (John 4:34). Jesus was obedient unto death.

I can't walk closely with God and walk in disobedience, too. No one can. It matters not how important we think the command God tells us to do is. Regardless of how we feel about it, whatever God tells us to do is of the utmost importance and deserves our full attention and focus and determination and hands-on work. Why? Because He said so! He alone is God. John 14:15 states, "If you love Me, you will keep my commandments." Simply put, if we love God, we will do what He tells us to do. Like walking in unforgiveness, the path of intimacy and the path of disobedience go in opposite directions.

Radical obedience brings radical blessings.

The biggest blessing there is in this life is to walk with the Lord.

Every time I say yes to God, I get closer and closer to Him.

I may not want to do everything He asks, but I do want to be closer to Him and He knows what is best for me. Psalm 18:30 states that God's ways are perfect.

Don't say no to God. Say yes.

Make a checklist. What are things has God commanded us to do in Scripture that you are not doing? What directions has He given you personally that you are not doing?

Pray about this list. Repent for being disobedient to Him. Ask the Lord to help you walk in radical (thorough, extreme) obedience to Him. Ask Him to condition and prepare your heart to say yes to Him before He even asks.

Start doing the things He has commanded of you, one by one. You may have more difficulty with some things than others, but He will strengthen you to do it. God will help you.

When God Is Silent

"But He answered her not a word ..." (Matthew 15:23)

God will be silent with us to develop deeper spiritual intimacy with Him.

When we are new believers in Christ, it seems like God goes out of His way to reveal His ways and His power in our lives. He answers prayers quickly, moving in response to our faintest cry or whisper like a mother with her newborn. We can see His movement in our lives so clearly!

As we grow in our walk, it appears as if He moves back some. He is like the loving parent who takes their child to school for the first time. It is frightening for the child at first, but sure enough the parent comes back at the end of the day to pick them up. Trials come in our lives, but God takes care of us, just as He promised.

Fast-forward some years. There may be times in your walk of spiritual intimacy with the Lord when it seems He is nowhere to be found. Your prayers bounce off the ceiling. God is quiet and it seems like He is far, far away.

Matthew 15:21–28 tells the story of a woman simply referred to as a woman of Canaan. She cries out to Jesus to help her daughter who is under satanic attack. Jesus says nothing, like she is not even there.

As I read the story, I can imagine her in my mind, begging and pleading. She is loud and demonstrative. So much so that she annoys the disciples, who ask Jesus to send her away.

Finally, He responds, "I'm not here for you" (paraphrase).

She comes closer and kneels before Him. "Lord! Master! Savior! Help me!"

He replies, "It would not be right to take the children's bread and give it to dogs." Yes, you heard that right. Jesus reminds her that she is a woman of Canaan, not a child of Israel. She is a dog, a Gentile. The blessings are not for her.

She presses on.

"Yes, Lord, you are right. I am a woman of Canaan. I'm a dog. But even dogs eat the crumbs that fall from the master's table. Lord, all I need is a crumb!" (paraphrase)

Jesus replies, "Woman, you have great faith! You shall have what you asked for." Her daughter is healed.

Let's review a few of the basic truths from this passage:

1. Jesus didn't have to respond to her cries (she was a Gentile), but in His grace and mercy, He did! I thank God that Jesus declared later that He had "other sheep too, that are not in this fold" (John 10:16). Paul stated, "you Gentiles, who were branches from a wild olive tree, have been grafted in. So now you also will receive the blessing God promised Abraham and his children" (Romans 11:17). I am thankful that now, there is neither Jew nor Gentile,

neither slave nor free, nor is there male and female, for you are all one in Christ Jesus. (Galatians 3:28)

2. Healing and deliverance are the children's bread. They are just a few of the blessings God has for those who belong to Him.

3. Jesus responds to faith in who He is and in what He can do! This woman, who was not a Jew, said, "Jesus, I know you. Nothing is too hard for you. Deliverance for my daughter is nothing for you to do. You are mighty in power. Healing is just a crumb. I don't have a right to the bread but that's all right, all I need is a crumb from you and my daughter will be healed! Hallelujah!" Is Jesus that big to you?

"Whosoever shall call upon the name of the Lord shall be saved." (Romans 10:13) "Whosoever" is a beautiful word. It means everyone is invited to have a spiritually intimate relationship with God.

In Scripture, there are times when God uses silence as a way of letting His people know He is displeased with them. The same is true today. When sin and disobedience is confessed, then fellowship with God can be restored.

God also uses silence to develop deeper spiritual intimacy with Him.

When it seems as if God is far away from us, He is more active in our lives than we can imagine. He is stretching our faith.

Two things are true: He loves us, and He will never leave or forsake us. It doesn't matter how we feel. God is always there. When you are with someone you are close to, you don't have to spend every second talking. You can just sit together and be quiet for long periods of time. The silence is not uncomfortable. You don't need constant reassurance that your relationship is okay, like you did when you first met. That's what God is doing in our walk with Him. He is helping us learn to trust Him when we don't hear Him or sense Him moving in our lives. We don't need to feel He is present; we simply know He is because He said He would be. He is faithful. In this season we learn to trust His Word and His promises regardless of what we see or feel. Spiritual intimacy between God and us grows. We grow.

God knows we need regular reassurance when we first come to know Him, but as we grow in our relationship with Him, He tries us with silence. When He answers not a word, He is right there! Don't back up. Don't listen to the lies of the enemy when he whispers to you that God doesn't see or hear you. Don't listen when the enemy of our souls says God doesn't love you. Like the woman of Canaan, press on. Keep praying. Don't stop talking to Him. Let God know you trust Him and that you are not going anywhere. When God is silent, He is calling us to an even deeper walk with Him based on a solid faith and not on feelings or circumstances. He'll speak and reveal Himself more clearly when it's time. In the meanwhile, don't back up! Press on!

"Ask and keep on asking and it will be given to you; seek and keep on seeking and you will find; knock and keep on knocking and the door will be opened to you. For everyone who keeps on asking receives, and he who keeps on seeking finds, and to him who keeps on knocking, it will be opened." (Matthew 7:7,8)

"The Lord Himself goes before you and will be with you. He will never leave you or forsake you. Do not be afraid; do not be discouraged." (Deuteronomy 31:8)

In Pursuit

John 20:1: *"The first day of the week cometh Mary Magdalene early, when it was yet dark, unto the sepulchre …"*

Mark 16:9: *"Now when Jesus was risen early the first day of the week, he appeared first to Mary Magdalene, out of whom he had cast seven devils."*

This is what pursuing Christ looks like.

Urgency

Love

Preparation

Expectancy

These words describe what an intimate relationship with Jesus looks like.

Mary Magdalene was at the crucifixion when the disciples ran away.

Now here she is early in the morning—while it was yet dark—to prepare Jesus' body for burial.

Jesus has been on her mind all night.

Have you ever been so concerned about doing something that it's hard to sleep the night before?

You are up and maybe even dressed before the alarm clock goes off.

This thing demands your immediate attention and you dare not wait a second longer than necessary.

I believe this describes the spirit Mary had that resurrection morning. I believe this is the spirit we are to have daily as we prepare to meet with God.

It must be of vital necessity that we are in His presence.

When something is important to us, when it's urgent, we don't let anything else get in the way. We don't say, "We'll see how the day goes ..." When it's that important, everything else is secondary.

That is the heart and mindset we are to have when it comes to spending time with God.

Why was it so important for her to prepare Jesus' body?

The key is in Mark 16:9.

"... He appeared first to Mary Magdalene, out of whom he had cast seven devils."

Seven devils?

In Scripture, the number seven represents completeness. The enemy had <u>complete</u> control over her life.

Can you imagine the torment Mary must have gone through? The pain, the hurt, the shame …

But then she met Jesus! He delivered her from *all* that. He came to set the captive free! (Luke 4:18) He met her greatest need when no one else could and probably wouldn't even dare to try.

He reached out to her in love when others probably went the opposite direction when they saw her coming.

For that she was grateful beyond words.

She loved Him.

When you think about the state you were in before Jesus came into your life … when you think about all He has done and is doing for you, you will run to Him.

Love causes us to run into His presence.

Mary Magdalene had an assignment. I'm sure she and the other women had everything they needed to prepare His body. Planning must have taken place.

Got that spice?
Who has the oil?
Where is the wrapping cloth?

They were ready.

It's the same way when it comes to spending time with God.

Poor preparation is a setup for failure.

Where is the spot you will meet Him for your appointment? You may have different places mapped out. Find out what place(s) work best for you.

Do you have paper and a pen, or some means to take notes? You may think "I could never forget a Scripture or something else that comes to me in prayer," but believe me, you can!

The spirit may be willing, but the flesh is just plain forgetful sometimes (to paraphrase the Scripture).

What time will you meet? If you don't set a time, it will never happen.

I used to say, "The Holy Spirit will wake me when I am to spend time with Him," and I didn't set a clock or anything. He would wake me, but I didn't always get up. ("What!? It's only 3:00 am!")

I had not prepared my mind to get up. Set an alarm if you need to. We set alarm clocks or timers on our phones for work, or if there is something important we need to do. What is more important than this?

More importantly, set your heart and mind to meet with Him. Ask God to help you.

Do you have your Bible? What else do you need?

Be prepared to meet with God so you can receive the blessing of time spent with Him.

He is ready to meet with you.

The virgins missed the wedding with the bridegroom.

Why?

They weren't prepared.

Mary expected to find Jesus' body to anoint for burial. When it was all over, she was one of the first to find Him gone; she spoke with angels and was the first to see and speak to the resurrected Lord!

WOW!

Would you say she saw and received more than she expected?

When you meet with the Lord, expect to hear from Him!

Expect to receive divine revelations!

Expect Him to answer your prayers!

Expect to be corrected! (The Lord chastises those He loves …)

Expect to be changed in His presence to look more like Him, to be changed on the inside!

Expect to be transformed!

"And now unto Him, who is able to do exceedingly abundantly above all we could ask or hope according to His power that works in us …" (Ephesians 3:20)

"The Lord's eyes run to and fro throughout the whole earth to shew Himself strong on behalf of those whose heart is loyal toward Him ..." (2 Chronicles 16:9)

He will do more than we could ever imagine as we seek to be close to Him.

Expect it.

***"To Him be glory in the church and in Christ Jesus throughout all generations for ever and ever! Amen."* (Ephesians 3:21)**

Share what God is doing in your life as you seek to make Him first at www.onethingfirst.org.

Scriptures

What does the Bible say about spiritual intimacy with God?

"But if from thence thou shalt seek the LORD thy God, thou shalt find [him], if thou seek him with all thy heart and with all thy soul." (Deuteronomy 4:29)

"I sought the Lord and He answered me and delivered me from all my fears." (Psalm 34:4)

"My heart has heard you say, 'Come and talk with me.' And my heart responds, 'LORD, I am coming.'" (Psalm 27:8)

"I love them that love me; and those that seek me early shall find me." (Proverbs 8:17)

"You will seek me and find me when you seek me with all your heart." (Jeremiah 29:13)

"Ask, and it shall be given you; seek, and ye shall find; knock, and it shall be opened unto you …" (Matthew 7:7)

"Seek the LORD and his strength, seek his face continually." (1 Chronicles 16:11)

"The LORD [is] good unto them that wait for him, to the soul [that] seeketh him." (Lamentations 3:25)

"Seek ye the LORD while he may be found, call ye upon him while he is near ..." (Isaiah 55:6)

"With my whole heart have I sought thee: O let me not wander from thy commandments." (Psalm 119:10)

"But seek ye first the kingdom of God, and his righteousness; and all these things shall be added unto you." (Matthew 6:33)

"But without faith [it is] impossible to please [him]: for he that cometh to God must believe that he is, and [that] he is a rewarder of them that diligently seek him." (Hebrews 11:6)

"The young lions do lack and suffer hunger: but they that seek the LORD shall not want any good [thing]." (Psalm 34:10)

"O God, thou [art] my God; early will I seek thee: my soul thirsteth for thee, my flesh longeth for thee in a dry and thirsty land, where no water is ..." (Psalm 63:1)

"Blessed [are] they that keep his testimonies, [and that] seek him with the whole heart." (Psalm 119:2)

"And they that know thy name will put their trust in thee: for thou, LORD, hast not forsaken them that seek thee." (Psalm 9:10)

"If my people, which are called by my name, shall humble themselves, and pray, and seek my face, and turn from their wicked ways; then will I hear from heaven, and will forgive their sin, and will heal their land." (2 Chronicles 7:14)

"The LORD looked down from heaven upon the children of men, to see if there were any that did understand, [and] seek God." (Psalm 14:2)

"Draw nigh to God, and he will draw nigh to you. Cleanse [your] hands, [ye] sinners; and purify [your] hearts, [ye] double minded." (James 4:8)

"... He is not far from every one of us ..." (Acts 17:27)

"... It is time to seek the LORD until He comes to rain righteousness on you ..." (Hosea 10:12)

"Evil men do not understand justice, but those who seek the LORD understand all things." (Proverbs 28:5)

"Glory in His holy name; Let the heart of those who seek the LORD be glad." (1 Chronicles 16:10)

Beginning a New Life in Christ

1. God loves us.

   John 3:16, "God so loved the world that He gave His one and only Son [Jesus Christ], that whosoever believes in Him shall not perish but have everlasting life."

2. We need a Savior to save us from the penalty of our sins, which is eternity in hell.

   Mankind is sinful. God is holy (right and perfect in every way). Sin separates us from God. "All have sinned and fall short of the glory of God." (Romans 3:23) We all need a Savior.

3. God sent Jesus to die for our sins.

   "God demonstrates His own love towards us in that while we were yet sinners, Christ died for us." (Romans 5:8)

   Jesus died and rose on the third day. He is the only way to God. Jesus, speaking, says: "I am the way, the truth and the life, no man comes to the Father, but through me!" (John 14:6).

"The wages of sin is death, but the gift of God is eternal life in Christ Jesus our Lord." (Romans 6:23)

There is only one true Savior—Jesus. "For there is one mediator between God and mankind, the man Christ Jesus." (1 Timothy 2:5)

4. We must repent, believe, and confess.

   Ask God to forgive you for your sins. Accept the death and resurrection of Jesus as payment for your sins. Accept Jesus as the Lord and Savior and the Lord of your life! Ask Him to lead, guide, and help you do what He wants you to do every day, starting right now. Thank Him for filling you with His Spirit.

   "If you openly declare that Jesus is Lord and believe in your heart that God raised him from the dead, you will be saved. For it is by believing in your heart that you are made right with God, and it is by openly declaring your faith that you are saved." (Romans 10:9 and 10)

5. Salvation is the first step of spiritual intimacy. Become part of a Bible-based Christian Church Fellowship for growth in your walk with God!

CPSIA information can be obtained
at www.ICGtesting.com
Printed in the USA
LVHW091115310521
688881LV00027B/328